If there are so few Croesuses left in our t...
there are so few, so very few, left who kn...
This is even more true on an island like ...
which has such rich and pure food
to offer the eyes you would say that
one would have to be mad
or without eyes to be left
unmoved by the light.

ODYSSEAS ELYTIS

TABLE OF CONTENTS

LESVOS

The island of Sappho

EDITIONS
TOUBI'S ®
ΕΚΔΟΣΕΙΣ

Texts: MIMI ELEFTHERIADI
Translation: Philip Ramp
Photographs: D.KOLIOPANOU, K. SYKAS, CHATZIDIMITRIOU   Archives: M. TOUBIS

Artistic Supervision, typesetting, colour separation, montage, printing: GRAPHIC ARTS MICHALIS TOUBIS S.A.

INTERNET: http://www.toubis.gr

2-200

TABLE OF CONTENTS

LESVOS

Lesvos, renowned since antiquity, is the island of harmony and dream. The flower of an eternal spring set on the blue waters of the Aegean, a vision that opens wide its modest beauty to the horizon, offering an invitation to love and promise. An ethereal substance you would say, made from the very breath of God. Matter that is moulded of a light made up of soft tones and sweet shadowing which emerges from the embrace of the sea and poised there achieves its equilibrium with the water, in a melding of myth and truth, contemplation and reality. As if the seasons had paused caught up in a feeling of responsibility and awe in the face of such beauty and then left this land pristine where the gods of joy and sun were worshipped and Sapphic grief was heard in the incomparable "Aeolian melody".

Thus, it is just as back then when the Tritons cavorted on the serene shores, when Cupids roamed in the brilliant gardens with flowers woven in their hair, when youth, in the figures of Daphnis and Chloe, spun the most tender tale of love that time has ever known. In this land beauty, the courtesy of true feeling, clear reasoning, passion for creation and longing for life cannot help but be in eternal bloom.

No discord. Even in the sheer cliffs plunging to the sea and the enormous masses of rock in the interior, in the dry stone walls and the ancient lava along the slopes, you will encounter a gentle pulse of tameness, a glow of meekness which gives you a feeling of intimacy, which draws near you, and enters you as a polite and welcome merging. Here is where song and lyric poetry, philosophical reflection and the arts first flowered, as ancient finds have shown. Homer mentions Lesvos as the seat of Makareos, the son of Helios, the most famed of the mythical kings. The poet Palamas said Lesvos was a temple to beauty and the novelist Myrivilis

thought of it as a flower-bedecked boat sailing between Greece and the Orient. Lesvos is a true princess of the deep blue Aegean. A hallucination. A myth. A truth. A paradise of serenity.

The island of harmony and dream

Mithymna, *woodcut, 62×91, 1971. Work by the painter-engraver K. Grammatopoulos.*

Mithymna has inspired artists since antiquity. Representatives of spiritual creation from throughout the world have come to the island in search of inspiration.

The beach at Skala Eressou.

The warm climate of the island, its fertile soil and abundant water, have created the lush green Lesvos that every visitor enjoys today. The ancient, boundless olive groves, the forests of pine, (the largest at Tsamliki), the thousands of varieties of plants and trees all make for an enchanting landscape such as the Spring of Karini and the "Garden of the Virgin Mary" (O Kipos tis Panayias). The animal kingdom of Lesvos has lived amid this vegetation for thousands of years while the marine flora and fauna await the more daring to come and enjoy them in the clean, rich sea around the island.

The climate of Lesvos is soft and temperate. Winter is mild and snowfall rare. The warm period on the island starts in April and lasts until October with little rainfall. The largest amount of rainfall, on a yearly average, is recorded in December and the least in July.

From a bioclimatic point of view Lesvos has a damp Mediterranean climate with generally warm winters. Lesvos was known in antiquity for its exceptionally fine Halcyon days, a period of warm summer-like light in the heart of winter, and this has continued right up to the present, with the sweet warm days of January and February.

The Roman historian Tacitus spoke of the island's climate as being, "noble and agreeable". There is more sunshine in Lesvos than practically any other place in Greece and, perhaps, in the whole Mediterranean. The island that during antiquity was noted for its worship of the god of light, Apollo, almost never, even in the dead of winter, does not at least briefly feel the sun's warm embrace.

Morphology - Therapeutic Springs - The Petrified Forest

LESVOS

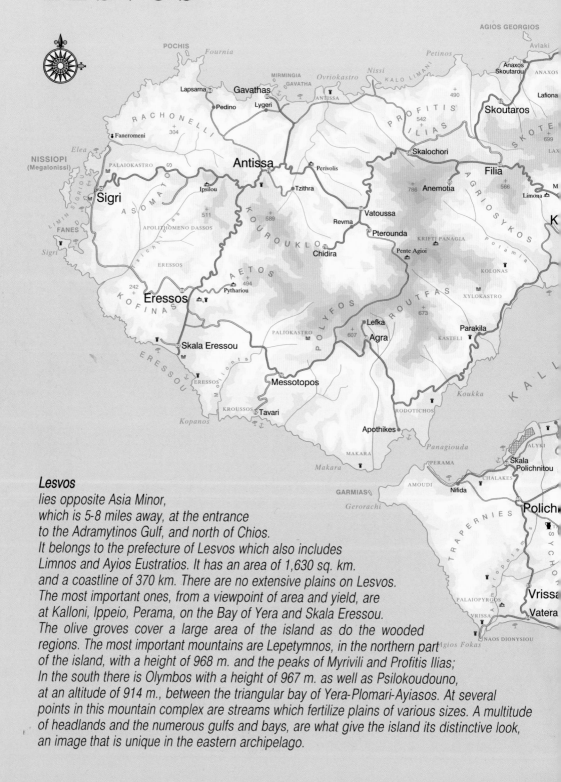

Molivo...
Mithimr
(Molivos

POCHIS *Fournia*
AGIOS GEORGIOS

Avlaki

MIRMINGIA *Ovriokastro*
GAVATHA *Nissi* Anaxos
Lapsarna **Gavathas** Skoutarou ANAXOS
Pedino Lygeri ANTISSA KALO LIMANI Lafiona

+ **Skoutaros**
490

R A C H O N E L L I + P R O F I T I S 542
+ I L I A S S K O T E...
304
‡ Faneromeni Skalochori + 699
Elea LAX

NISSIOPI **Antissa** 786 Anemotia **Filia** +
(Megalonissi) PALAIOKASTRO Perivolis + 566
Ipsilou Tzithra M
Sigri A S O M A T O S A G R I O S Y K O S Limona...

LIMIN SIGRIOU 511 Vatoussa K
FANES + Revma KRIFTI PANAGIA
589 Pterounda Potamia
APOLITHOMENO DASSOS K O U R O U K L O...
Sigri Pente Agioi
ERESSOS Chidira KOLONAS
A E T O S + XYLOKASTRO
494
K O F I N A S Pythariou P O L Y F O S 673
242 R O U T F A S
+ Lefka Parakila
Eressos PALIOKASTRO + **Agra** KASTELI
607
E R E S S O U Skala Eressou
Messotopos RODOTICHOS Koukka K A L L...
ERESSOS KROUSSOS Tavari
Kopanos Apothikes Panagiouda
MAKARA PERAMA ALYKI
Makara AMOUDI Nifida CHALAKES Skala
GARMIAS Polichnitou
Gerorachi **Polich**

T R A P E R N I E S P S Y C H R O...

Vrissa
PALAIOPYRGOS **Vatera**
VRISSA
Agios Fokas
NAOS DIONYSIOU

Lesvos
lies opposite Asia Minor,
which is 5-8 miles away, at the entrance
to the Adramytinos Gulf, and north of Chios.
It belongs to the prefecture of Lesvos which also includes
Limnos and Ayios Eustratios. It has an area of 1,630 sq. km.
and a coastline of 370 km. There are no extensive plains on Lesvos.
The most important ones, from a viewpoint of area and yield, are
at Kalloni, Ippeio, Perama, on the Bay of Yera and Skala Eressou.
The olive groves cover a large area of the island as do the wooded
regions. The most important mountains are Lepetymnos, in the northern part
of the island, with a height of 968 m. and the peaks of Myrivili and Profitis Ilias;
In the south there is Olymbos with a height of 967 m. as well as Psilokoudouno,
at an altitude of 914 m., between the triangular bay of Yera-Plomari-Ayiasos. At several
points in this mountain complex are streams which fertilize plains of various sizes. A multitude
of headlands and the numerous gulfs and bays, are what give the island its distinctive look,
an image that is unique in the eastern archipelago.

Efthalou

Skala
Sikamias

Argenos

Lepetimnos

Sikamia

Korakas

Faros

PALAIOKASTRO

Tsonia

MIRIVILI
EPETIMNOS

Vafios

968

Kapi

Klio

Limani

ANEMOMYLOS

Koukmidos

Palios

Tsakmaki

Pelopi

MAVRADIA

Taxiarchis

LAXEFTI TAFI

PANAGIAS

Stipsi

Ypsilometopo

PALAIOCHRISTIANIKI

Madamados

Agios Stefanos

Agios Stefanos

BARBALIAS

ASPRONISSOS

TSOUKALAS

Napi

AVDELLAS

324

MAKRI GIALOU

PRASSOLOGOS

Xampelia

Agia Paraskevi

Palaiochristianikos
Naos Chalinadou

KYDONAS

Marangos

S APOLLONAS

371

Tsikniàs

MYLOPOTAMOS

MESSA

Nees Kidonies

Skala
Neon Kidonion

GLIKI SKALA

NAOS MESSON

TAVROS

Skala
Mistegnon

Mistegna

EGYROS

Agioi Akindinoi

MISSINTZIKI

DASSOS PEFKON
TSAMLIKI

Komi

447

Pigi

PETRES TOU ARAPI

Agios Georgios

PIRPA

MAVRACHIA

Achladeri

Agios Rafail

Thermi

Paralia Thermis
Petralonia
Panagia
Trouloti
Pyrgoi Thermis

THERMI

SPATHI

Lampou
Myloi

ROMAIKO YDRAGOGIO

451

Pamfilla

Paralia

PAMFILIA

STENOKLIDI

APPIDOVOUNO

Keramia

Afalonas

Karalepes

ssilika

Ipion

LOUTRO KORFOU

Moria

Panagiouda

ROMAIKO YDRAGOGIO

LOUTRA KOURTZI

Pigi Tsingou

Asomatos

KASTELLI

Sykounda

Agioi Anargyroi

Outza

ARCHAIO THEATRO

PROFITIS

Agiassos

GERAS

PIGADAKIA

Kedro

Alifanta

MYTILINI
(Chora)

OLYMBOS

968

Ampeliko

Sanatorio

Mychos

Kato Tritos

Pyrgi

Sourada

Stavros

XYLOKASTRO

NAPI

Chalikas

Koumikon

Varia

Akothi

Akrotiri

Kato Stavros

PSILOKOUDOUNO

Evriaki

Neapolis

Akrasi

Neochori

845

Plakados

Palaiokipos

Koudouroudia

Taxiarches

Pligoni

Agia Marina

Drota

914

Papados

Chalatses

PALAIOCHRISTIANIKI

RODITIS

Megalochori

Messagros

Perama

Loutra

AIRPORT

Palaiochori

Skopelos

PRINOVOUNI

580

Messouna

Marmaro

Skala Loutron

KOURTER

488

Kratigos

NAGIA KRIFTI

Kournella

PSIFIDIA

Agios Ermogenis

AMALI

Agios
Georgios

Melinda

ANGATERI

Kato Chorio

Milies

Pyrgoi

Aftelia
(Kavourolimni)

Maleas
(Agrilia)

Plomari

Trygonas

Plagia

MIRSSINA

Kefalos

Agios
Isidoros

KASTRI

Tarti

FTELIA

MERSINIA

AGIOS VASSILIOS

Airport

Archaeological Sites

Monasteries

Castles

Caves

Therapeutic Springs

The boundless olive groves are intersected by lush pine forests, stands of oak, chestnut and plane trees, as well as myrtle, laurel and wild olive and a vast variety of aromatic plants which cover all of Lesvos.

The essence of beauty permeates every corner. The feeling of tranquillity and harmonious proportion is all around you. Beauty is a constant companion. In the mountain cataracts. In the waterways. Under the cool shade of the eternal trees. In the deep silence of dusk. In the hot, calm mornings. In the silver bays where ancient civilizations have come and gone. In the crystal-clear summer nights. In the cascading vegetation whose spread is only checked by the shores themselves and the bare clearings.

The Therapeutic Springs of Lesvos

Nature gave yet another gift to Lesvos: the therapeutic springs which are scattered throughout the island, the remnants of ancient volcanic activity in that area and the proof of it. Their mineral, sodium chloride and radioactive rich water, the variety of temperatures and the units of radioactivity in that water have been famed in Lesvos since antiquity and attract a large number of visitors to the island.

Today, at Ayiassos, Lisvori, Thermi, Loutra, Eftalou and Argennos, there are therapeutic springs with a very good tourist infrastructure, which are suitable for nearly all kinds of therapy. This wealth, which is located at lovely coastal sites or in verdant landscapes, makes Lesvos perhaps the most beautiful place for therapy in the Mediterranean.

The abundant vegetation goes right down to the shore. Everywhere one has the feeling of serenity, beauty and measure.

The Petrified Forest of Lesvos

Between 15 and 20 million years ago Lesvos was
covered with tropical and subtropical forests,
which was unique for Greece not to mention the
whole Mediterranean, This singular vegetation was
the result of many underground deposits of water
which the island still has today but was primarily due
to the active volcanoes which existed then (though at
locations unknown to us today). These rain-forests,
with their enormous trees, which today
can still be found in SE Asia and California, were
suddenly covered with lava and volcanic ash,
after intense volcanic activity. The water that filtered
through this earth of volcanic origin for thousands
of years petrified the trunks of the trees, and the
plants and animals that were covered. The petrified
trees that have survived to the present, in an area
of approximately 40,000 acres in the NW part of the
island, are made up mainly of quartz and opal, while
the characteristics of the trees are easy to see, such
as the growth rings and the bark. The Petrified Forest
has been proclaimed a "Monument of Nature Subject
to Preservation" and most of it is open to the visitor.

3

HISTORY
Antiquity - Byzantinum - Modern Times

According to the myths, the island was first populated by the descendants of Makareos, the son of Helios (the sun). This mythical king, had five daughters: Mytilene, Methymna, Issa, Antissa and Arisve and four sons: Eressos, Kydrolaos, Neandros and Leukippos. It is from these children of Makareos that the principal towns of Lesvos later took their names. One of the sons-in-law of the king was Lesvos, son of the Thessalian hero Lapithos and it was from him that the island took its name.

The marble throne of the orator Potamon (Archaeological Museum of Mytilene).

Another explanation is that the name Lesvos means an island with lush vegetation and captivating, attractive natural beauty.

The beginnings of the history of Lesvos are lost in the mists of time, but its seems it was inhabited as far back as the fourth millennium B.C. Homer mentions Lesvos in both The "**Iliad**" and The "**Odyssey**". It was here that Achilles and Ajax buried Palamides, the hero of the Trojan War who invented writing, numbers and weights and measures. After the fall of Troy, it was on Lesvos that Menelaus, Diomides and Odysseus met to decide the manner of their return home.

As the discoveries of archaeology have shown, a civilization parallel to that of Troy and Mycenae developed on Lesvos.

Archaic - Classical times (1100-88 B.C.)

In 1100 - 1000 B.C., some sixty years after the fall of Troy, an Aeolian colony was established on Lesvos by Kras, of the Penthilids. Mytilene flourished and gradually extended its commercial and colonial activities to the shores of Asia Minor opposite, which took the name Mytilenean Aegialos (Mytilenean "shore"). It was in this area, near the tomb of Achilles, that the inhabitants of Mytilene built the town of Achilleion. In 659 B.C. the Penthilos dynasty came to an end when the people of Mytilene revolted and murdered the last of the Penthilid tyrants. The inhabitants of Lesvos turned to agriculture and shipping, and Lesvos was a major naval power for a considerable length of time. In 570 B.C. Lesvos set up a Greek trading station in Egypt. In 492 these people were themselves conquered by the Persians. Lesvos threw off the Persian yoke in 479 and participated as an equal in the Attic-Eleian Alliance. During the Peloponnesian War, the inhabitants of Lesvos, with the exception of the residents of Methymna, seceded from the Athenian alliance and took the side of Sparta. In June of 427 Mytilene fell to the Athenians.

In 415 B.C. the Methymnian fleet joined with the Athenians in the expedition against Syracuse. In 405 Lesvos was taken by the Spartans under Lysander, but was retaken by the Athenians in 389. Between 395-387 it took part in the Corinthian War. In 385 it again came under Spartan dominance but in 375 joined the second Athenian alliance. In 334 B.C., following the Battle of the Granicus, the Mytilenians allied themselves with Alexander the Great. It was during this period that the brothers Erigyos and Laomedon, sons of Larichos of Lesvos, who had been childhood friends of Alexander, came to prominence. Laomedon had an excellent knowledge of Asiatic languages and was employed on confidential missions during the campaign in Asia Minor. After the death of Alexander the Great, he assumed control of the satrapy of Syria. Erigyos was put in charge of the allied cavalry during the expedition. In 323 B.C., after the death of Alexander, Lesvos came under the rule of the Ptolemies.

Roman period *(88 B.C. - 324 A.D.)*

In 88 B.C. Lesvos was conquered by the Romans. In the various battles that occurred during the siege of Mytilene, the young Julius Caesar distinguished himself by his bravery.

The orator Cicero, speaking from the rostrum of the Roman Senate on the subject of this further success of Roman arms, described Mytilene as a town with fine buildings and fertile fields.

In 62 B. C. Mytilene was visited by Pompey and the inhabitants held magnificent games in his honor. Pompey, who numbered among his friends the historian Theophanes of Mytilene, granted the town self-government. In 48 B.C., following the battle of Pharsala, Pompey visited Mytilene for a second time. This period was marked by the presence of the sophist and rhetorician Lesbonax, father of Potamon, who was also an orator, the orator Lesbocles and the epigrammatic poet Krinagoras. Strabo lists them among the great men of Mytilene. Krinagoras was sent as the ambassador of Mytilene to Rome, on two occasions, and managed to obtain privileges for the town's inhabitants from Julius Caesar. In 52 A. D. St. Paul visited Lesvos. In 70 A.D., during the reign of the emperor Vespasian, Lesvos again became a Roman province and its privileges were abolished. It recovered them under the Emperor Hadrian.

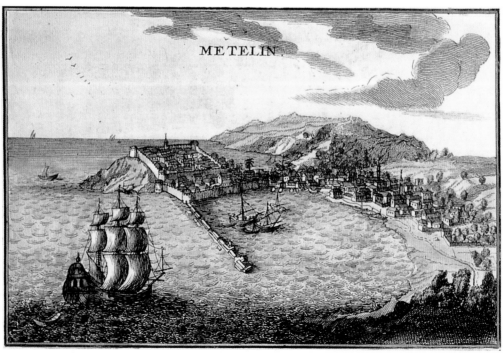

METELIN.

Byzantine period (324 - 1453)

After the division of the Roman Empire into Eastern and Western sections, Lesvos became part of the Eastern or Byzantine Empire. Throughout the history of the Byzantine state the island was used as a place of exile for persons of note, such as Irene the Athenian, Symeon Magister, Constantine VIII Monomachos, to name but a few. The year 851 A.D. saw the beginning of repeated Saracen attacks on Lesvos. The island was then plundered by the Venetians and the Crusaders. It passed successively to the Latin Empire and to Nicaea before finally returning to Byzantine rule in 1261.

Exhibits from the Byzantine and Ecclesiastical Museum of Mytilene.

Rule of the Gattelusi (1354-1462)

In 1354 Lesvos was given as a dowry to the Genoese nobleman Francesco Gattelusi, son-in-law of the Emperor John Palaeologos, who came to the island with his wife Maria in 1355. Francesco Gattelusi ruled until 1376 and was succeeded by Giacomo Gattelusi, Nicola Gattelusi, as regent for the minor Dorino Gattelusi, Dorino Gattelusi, Domenico Gattelusi and Nicola Gattelusi. In 1373 the castle was renovated by Francesco Gattelusi. There is an inscription to that effect built into the wall above the large gate. In 1401 the island was badly damaged by an earthquake and Francesco Gattelusi died under the ruins of his palace. In 1445 the apostate Bulgar Baldaoglou plundered Lesvos and razed to the ground the town of Kalloni, which had been enjoying remarkable economic prosperity until then.

In 1462 Mohamet II the Conqueror attacked Mytilene. On 1 September of that year he besieged it by sea. At the time the town contained twenty thousand inhabitants, of whom fifteen thousand were non-combatants and five thousand under arms. The Sultan brought up large numbers of infantry and a large fleet.

The Turks attempted to take the fortifications of the castle by frontal attack, but they were forced to fall back with heavy losses caused by the rocks rolled down on them by the besieged. On the fourth day of the siege the inhabitants of Mytilene broke out and drove the Turks far from their walls. However, their momentum was so great that they swept all the way to the Turkish camp where they found themselves faced with superior forces and were decimated. On the fifth day the Turks launched a heavy attack. The castle was badly damaged by the bombardment. The ramparts of Mytilene were put out of action one by one and the walls were breached at many points. Nicola Gattelusi, seeing that further resistance was hopeless, proposed to Mahmout Pasha a surrender of the castle, but on condition that he would be granted other land to live on. The proposal was communicated to the Sultan who accepted it. He himself disembarked from his ship at Mytilene and took up residence in a magnificent tent at Epano Skala, near the castle. To this place he summoned Nicola Gattelusi and the treaty was signed the Sultan making it one of his terms that the whole island was to be surrendered to him and its fortresses disarmed. On October 14 Lesvos became subject to Mohamet II.

Turkish Occupation (1462-1817)

What followed beggars description. The Sultan gave orders that all the inhabitants, men, women and children, should be paraded before him as he sat on his throne surrounded by bodyguards and officers. Parents, couples, and brothers and sisters were parted in the most inhuman manner, in accordance with the conquerors' interests. Eight hundred beautiful or strong looking boys and girls, were sent to Constantinople to fill the Sultan's harem, and the ranks of the Janassaries. The town was plundered and of the hundred thousand inhabitants the island had at the time of the Gattelusi, all that remained were thirty thousand illiterate paupers. Many were sold into slavery while others moved, either compulsorily or voluntarily, to Constantinople. The Sultan also broke the treaty. Instead of letting Gattelusi go free, he threw him into prison, together with his brother Lucino where, after they had renounced Christianity, they were hanged with a bowstring, in the same way that they themselves had hanged Domenico Gattelusi four years previously. The sword of the conqueror divides the history of the island with a line of blood. However, from amid the ruins and the ashes, as though driven by some hidden extremely ancient force, the first small rallying points, dedicated to the survival and the continuation of Hellenism, started to form.

Secret schools began to operate in the churches and monasteries and, as in the rest of occupied Greece, the clergy played a leading part in keeping alive the hope for national regeneration.

The harbor of Mytilene in a copperplate.

During the period of the Turkish occupation Lesvos was raided by the Venetians and the Russians and was used as a place of exile for patriarchs and leading Turks who had fallen into disfavor with the Sultan.

In 1677 the castle of Mytilene was repaired and in 1757 the Turks built the castle of Sigri to protect the area from raiders. During the Russo-Turkish War of 1768-1774, Lesvos assumed the role of the first line of defense for the Hellespont, as Mohamet had foreseen. The irregulars who accompanied the Russians attempted to loot the island, and in revenge the Turks slaughtered the Christians. On the signing of the Treaty of Kuchuk-Kainarji, which put an end to the war, a period of increased prosperity began for Lesvos, after a hiatus of nearly 2,000 years.

This treaty stipulated that there should be freedom of religion for the enslaved Christian Greeks and gave Russia the right to intervene on behalf of the Church, which at that time was the link that bound all subject Greek people together. Trade was developed and direct, continuous contact was established with other Greek colonies. This was how the new ideas that would pave the way for the uprising against the oppressor, found their way to the island.

Revolutionary movements (1817-1912)

In 1817 one hears of the first members of the "Philiki Etaireia" (literally, "Friendly Society"). One of its members was the merchant Palaeologos Lemonis, who was initiated into the Society by Emmanuel Xanthos.

In 1821 Dimitrios Papanikolis used his fireships to blow up the Turkish frigate "Moving Mountain" in the waters off Eressos. The Turks in revenge slaughtered large numbers of Christians.

Because of its geographical position, Lesvos was the base of operations and the refuge of the Turkish fleet throughout the course of the struggle for Greek independence. An uprising of the inhabitants of Mytilene in 1824 was bloodily put down by the Turks.

In 1826 the Greek naval captain Miaoulis defeated the Turkish fleet in the straits of Mytilene and pursued it as far as Smyrna. In 1867 there was a major earthquake on the island in which a thousand people were killed and the town of Mytilene severely damaged.

Liberation
World War II (1912-1944)

On the morning of 8 November 1912, Mytilene was liberated by a squadron of the Greek fleet which arrived in the waters off the island, together with the battleship Averof. Admiral Koundouriotis called upon the Turks to surrender the town within two hours. The Turkish military governor asked for twenty-four hours in order to have time to consult Constantinople. Koundouriotis refused. He allowed only one more hour's grace. Before long the landing of the Greek troops on the stone steps began and the Greek flag was raised on the Turkish government building and the castle amid general rejoicing. The Turkish army withdrew to the interior. The liberation of the island was completed at the Battle of Klapados (4-8 December 1912). The Turkish army was defeated and forced to surrender.

On Tyrannidi Hill there is a memorial to the Greeks who fell in the battle, while in a small building on the right side of the road to Petra there are photocopies of the relevant documents housed on the spot where the act of surrender was signed. Lesvos was finally ceded to Greece by the Treaties of London and Athens in 1914.
Greek rights to the island were recognized by the Treaties of Sevres and Lausanne in 1923 when, with the exchange of populations, the last Turks left the island. During the Second World War the German occupation of the island began 4 May 1941. The island again became free on 10 September 1944.

The renowned Castle of Mytilene.

4

CULTURE & TRADITION

Customs - Feasts & Festivals - Music & Dances
Traditional Costumes - Arts & Letters - Architecture - Museums

The island of Lesvos is a richly endowed land both by nature and its inhabitants. Its natural beauties, its climate and its fertile soil have given birth to a people with a profound sense of beauty and harmony, from the depths of antiquity right up to the present. It is not by chance that even during mythological times Lesvos was known for its flourishing arts. When Orpheus, the great musician and poet was killed in Thrace, it is said that his lyre was swept away by the waters of the Evros river and carried to the shores of Lesvos where the inhabitants found it and put it in a temple, a place where music and poetry were worshipped. Since then it is said that even the nightingales of Lesvos sing more sweetly and melodiously than any other spot on earth. So this area has given birth too and nourished

"Limnian Shepherd" by the great folk painter, Theophilos.

poets the like of Sappho and Alcaeus in antiquity and Odysseas Elytis in our time, prose writers such as Myrivilis and philosophers such as Pittacus and Theophrastus and painters the likes of G. Lakovidis and Theophilos and countless others besides. Furthermore, it is not by chance that the representatives of spiritual creation from throughout the world come to the island in search of inspiration, the beautiful. This spiritual wealth and the need for artistic and intellectual creation is passed down from generation to generation through the living traditions of the island in music, song, dance, the inhabitants' occupations and way of life. These traditions are the distillation of millennia of wisdom and direct the present course of the island down through time.

People and occupations

It is with true originality that the inhabitants of Lesvos have confronted the changes brought to their lives by modern development and tourism. They have retained their manners and customs along with religious piety, especially in the interior of the island, but they are in no way standoffish with visitors.

On the contrary, it would be hard to find a place with so many hospitable people who are sure of their way of life and have much to tell you, without being afraid of the new. The traditional way of life on Lesvos is not opposed to progress but it distils each new thing and purifies it before it is embodied in the daily life of the island's inhabitants.

The natural wealth of Lesvos, with its fertile
soil and teeming sea, has for centuries
now supported all those who work with
traditional means.
Farmers, shepherds, potters, woodworkers
and so many others, take the island's gifts and
make them into small works of art and, in the
evening, they will talk to you about all that like an
old friend in the small, picturesque cafes.

Customs

Through their close links to the past, the people of Lesvos have kept up many traditional customs. In numerous villages the Christmas tree is not a fir but an olive branch decorated with gilded oranges, nuts and toys. On New Year's Day the young men and women go to the spring and fetch water, without saying a word. They sprinkle their houses with this "speechless" water. The men smash a pomegranate on the doorsteps of their houses, while holding a piece of iron in their hands. The pomegranate symbolizes abundance and wealth and the iron health. In the Plomari district an olive branch is hung over the outside doors in the belief that this will ensure a good supply of olive oil. At the midnight service on Easter, the Bishop, standing on a special platform, drinks wine from a silver cup which he then throws to the crowd which packs the yard of the Cathedral Church. Whoever catches the cup receives a gift of money from the Bishop, together with some Easter eggs. The Metropolitan also presents colored Easter eggs to the representatives of the Authorities and to the crowds which converge on his residence to greet him with the traditional words "Christ is risen". This custom has been observed since the time of the Turkish occupation. The same custom has been kept up in Plomari while on Good Friday it is customary for the different processions bearing the decorated bier of Christ to meet in the large square by the sea where the candles held by the thousands of worshippers create an otherworldly atmosphere. Furthermore, another rare custom has survived, found primarily in Panayiouda but also in Skala Kallonis and several other villages; this is the "To Kapsimo tou Ovriou", the "Burning of Judas" on the evening of Christ's Resurrection.

Carnival costumes in the village of Mesotopos.

Feasts and Festivals

A major festival for the whole of Lesvos takes place on 15 August at Ayiassos, a mountain village on the slopes of Mt. Olympos, where there is an impressive church dedicated to the Panayia (Virgin Mary), whose feast-day it is. Thousands of pilgrims converge on the village and its streets turn into one big fair with a full range of folk art, while in the evening things heat up in the night spots with dancing, eating and drinking and the sounds of traditional instruments. Hundreds of pilgrims from all over Greece, and even from abroad, come to Ayiassos on 15 August, in the fulfilment of a vow and to pay homage to the icon of the Virgin Mary.

Another festival involving the whole island is the one held on the third Sunday after Easter at Mantamados on the anniversary of the dedication of the magnificent Church of the Taxiarch (The Archangel), who is regarded to be the patron saint of Lesvos.

The festival is marked by the holding of a fair and the sacrifice of an animal. This is an old custom going back to the time of the Turkish occupation and is considered to be a relic of ancient paganism. On the eve of the feast the animal, which is donated by a leading citizen, or citizens, is first blessed by the priest, and then loaded with gold ornaments and flowers before being slaughtered. The meat is cooked in great cauldrons over open-air fires together with wheat and is served to the pilgrims. An observance involving many folk and pagan elements is the Feast of the Bull held on the last Sunday in May in the town of Ayia Paraskevi and dates back to 1774.

The animal destined to be sacrificed here is also provided by the rich and devout natives of the town. It is decked out and paraded through the town with great pomp, preceded by a band playing traditional instruments. Members of the Farmers' Cooperative which organizes the event, pass round offertory plates into which men and women throw money in fulfilment of a vow. It is customary for them to touch the animal since it is believed that contact brings good fortune.

It begins on the preceding Thursday with the procession described above. On the Friday the officials of the Cooperative set out for the distant point of Tavros ("Bull") together with a number of their colleagues and their wives, riding simply decorated horses. The husband of the leading couple holds the flag and his wife the icon of the saint. A folk band takes them round the market place and then accompanies them to the hamlet of Kafkara, where the priest, the team with the necessary equipment and the animal to be sacrificed awaits them. From there they set out for Tavros where the peddlers with their festive merchandise and the musicians for the celebrations have already arrived. On the Saturday morning marvelously decked out domestic animals with polished saddles, silvered chest bands and multi-colored beads stand ready in the streets. The villagers ride the horses, treat one another to drinks in the cafes and, when they have reached a state of high spirits, set off for Kafkara. From there they take the path to Tavros. Waiting for them there at the picturesque little chapel of the saint is the priest in his gold vestments.

The pilgrims arrive in groups, climb the steps up the rock leading to the chapel and receive the priest's blessing.

The sacrifice takes place in the evening. The priest reads a prayer and this is followed by the auctioning of the right to perform the sacrifice. Large sums are bid by many who have undertaken a vow. The highest bidder traces a cross on the throat of the beast with a knife and then it is slaughtered by a professional butcher. The pilgrims daub a cross on their forehead and the palms of their hands with its blood, another ancient custom. The whole of that Saturday evening is given over to merrymaking under the pine trees while the "keskesi" the meat of the animal mixed with wheat, onions and spices, is left to cook all night. The woods echo with music and song. On Sunday morning, following a festal mass in the chapel, the "keskesi" is divided up and the midday food and drink is served.

After that the groups of pilgrims set off for home. At Stalos, a short distance outside the village, the locals will have gathered to await the pilgrims. Here spectacular races are held in the evening. Professional riders are not permitted to enter these races. The winners are awarded valuable prizes. Later the pilgrims, led by the victors, visit the houses of relatives and friends where they are welcomed and exchange greetings.

The "Tavros" festival is based on a beautiful legend:

"During the time of the Turkish occupation a farmer from Ayia Paraskevi, called Malomytis, lost his ox. In his search for it he entered the domain of a Turkish bandit who attempted to kill him. Every time, however, that he was about to pull the trigger, his human target vanished from before his very eyes. The Turk attributed this miracle to Ayios Charalambos, the saint who was venerated in that area.

He left his cover, approached the Christian, gave him back his ox, for it was he who had stolen it, and told him to light a candle to the saint because he had saved him. Malomytis, profoundly moved, returned to his village and told the village elders of the miracle. The priest and the elders took the icon of the saint and set off for the mountain called "Tavros". Shortly afterwards the Turks, having seen the lights lit by the Christians, arrived in an angry mood. But they came to accept the explanation they were given and permitted a service to be held, telling the elders they could come every year to honor their saint, without fear."

Many Greeks and foreigners pay a special visit to Ayia Paraskevi in order to study and record this unusual festival.

A similar service, with the same significance, is also performed at the villages of Pigi and Napi. A major festival also takes place at Petra on 15 August in honor of the Virgin Mary. Here too meat is cooked with wheat and served to the worshippers who come from various parts of the island and from even further afield, and include many foreigners.

Music - Dances

The dance is the the way the people of Lesvos express their optimism and rejoicing. Young men and women dance in traditional costume, with grace and vigor, on joyful occasions and at festivals, the "Lesviakos" and the "Mytileniakos" dances connected to the local climate, and are the product of the island's open spirit which longs for light and free expression. The "batos" is danced by couples, a young man and woman, and its graceful movements are said to be in imitation of the courtship dances of pigeons. The dances performed in lines which face each other are the most characteristic on the island and are accompanied by this song:

On the island of Lesvos the songs always echo
Through the green olive groves
Willowy girls, smiling sweetly
Pluck daisies, violets and anemones.

Music is innate to the people of Lesvos. Folk bands lend a lively note of celebration and optimism to festivals and other happy events of life. The past in all its beauty is brought to life again by the local musicians and singers, in houses and cafes, in the open air and in the winter meeting places, an example of the islander's devotion to his splendid traditions.

1. Folk instrument player.
2. Dance and festival event.
3. 4. Traditional costumes from Mytilene.

Folk Costumes

Many of the typical, traditional costumes
of Lesvos have been preserved and can be seen
in a permanent exhibition organized by the
Lesvos Women's Association.
Men's garments for feast-days and weddings,
but also for everyday wear, woollen capes, furs,
overcoats and trousers, women's costumes,
gold-embroidered costumes from Plomari, Vrisa,
Yera and the northern villages and woven silk
garments are all to be found in this extremely
interesting exhibition of the traditional costume
of Lesvos. In the same exhibition, the Association
has on display the island's traditional weaving
and embroidery. This contains pure silk weavings
with delicate colors and charming designs
examples of the dedicated hard work of the girls
who wove the contents of their dowries
on the loom. Folk collections with the costumes
of Lesvos, each with its own unique exhibits,
can be found throughout the island and are
open to visitors all year round.

35

Arts and Letters

Literature has flourished on Lesvos during many periods, from antiquity to the present. It has been said the island enjoyed the favor of the Muses as a way of explaining its exceptional cultural development. It was the inhabitants of Lesvos who, according to tradition, buried with honors the head of Orpheus, son of the muse Calliope, when it washed up on the shore of Antissa. Orpheus had been torn apart by the Maenads of Thrace for not deigning to worship them after the death or Eurydice, and was then thrown into the river Evros. Together with the head of Orpheus the waves also bore to Lesvos his lyre, and since that time the nightingales of the island have been said to sing more sweetly there than anywhere else in the world. The famous philosopher and botanist Theophrastes (372-287 B.C.) was a native of Eressos. He studied with Plato and Aristotle and carried on their work. He was a Peripatetic and his writings deal with Metaphysics, Logic, Politics, Ethics, Poetry and the Physical Sciences. He also wrote many works on plants and has been called the father of Botany.

The historian Theophanes was born at Mytilene about 100 B.C. He accompanied Pompey on his military operations in Asia Minor and wrote an account of them. Pompey, in return for his services, accorded him the rights of a Roman citizen. Theophanes made use of Pompey's favor for the benefit of his native town, Mytilene, which Pompey on his return from Asia in 62 B.C. proclaimed free and then lavishly ornamented. The inhabitants of Mytilene honored Theophanes by striking coins with the inscription, "Theophanes, god of the Mytileneans".

The renowned musician and poet Arion (625-595 B.C.) came from Methymna and was called "Methymneaus". He lived chiefly at the court of the tyrant of Corinth Periander, where he acquired a great reputation. He was responsible for the reform of the dithyramb and thus contributed to the development of tragedy. A charming story is told about him and his lyre: when he was returning from Tarrentum on a Corinthian ship, his wealth provoked the envy of the sailors to the point where they plotted to throw him overboard.

He asked that he be allowed to first play something on his lyre. His song attracted a large dolphin to the ship which was so delighted with his singing that it took him on its back and carried him safely to Taenarum.

Terpander, the great musician and creator of choral poetry, was born at Antissa around 710 B.C. In his attempt to create more complex music he perfected the cithara, giving it seven strings instead of the three it had had. During his lifetime his fame was very great and a number of legends attached themselves to his character. We are told that after the Messenian War he was invited to Sparta, where he succeeded in putting an end to internecine feuding with his music.

Mytilene was the birthplace of one of the Seven Sages of Antiquity, Pittacus, who was born there in 648 B.C. Allying himself with the aristocratic party, he succeeded in bringing about the fall of the ruling tyrant. He became a general and fought against the Athenians at Signeum. In 595-594 he was vested with dictatorial powers; the inhabitants of Mytilene elected him "aesymnetes", a kind of elected tyrant, and as such he ruled for ten years. He introduced and applied new laws, granted an amnesty to his enemies, among whom was the poet Alcaeus, since he believed that forgiveness was better than punishment. On his decision to relinquish power, the Mytileneans presented him with a piece of land, the "Pittacan plot" from which he took an area no larger than the distance he could throw his spear, for, as he said, "a fair amount is more than enough". Many coins of ancient Mytilene have his portrait in relief and the inscription: "PHITTAKOS".

Sappho and Alcaeus, two figures who stand out with particular brilliance in the ancient world, were both natives of Lesvos. Both belong to the 6th century B.C. and both were leading representatives of the Aeolian school of lyric poetry. Sappho remains unrivalled, even today, for the passion, the sensitivity and the subtle lyric vibrancy of her lines.

Sappho's "Death Leap"
into the sea (copperplate).

Plato called her the tenth Muse, and one of her poems, so delighted Solon that, it is said, he wished to recite it from memory just before he died. Sappho was born at Eressos in 612 B.C. Political disturbances made her leave for Sicily, together with the supporters of the aristocratic faction. A few years later she returned to Lesvos. She devoted herself to the education of the young women of Mytilene by founding a school where she taught music, poetry and etiquette. This school was also attended by young women from the shores of Asia Minor opposite. Progressive ideas were prevalent in the Lesvos of that period and women were regarded as individuals with their own independent existence. Sappho's concern with the good conduct of the girls and women filled a social need felt by the aristocracy of Lesvos which laid great emphasis on poetry and music as accomplishments suited to a woman's education. The poetry of Sappho is marked by a warmth of feeling and spontaneity combined with the passion which is a hallmark of the Aeolian school. The shadow cast over her character and morals by the Athenian comic poets is due, it is believed, to a misunderstanding on their part, since they were not in a position to appreciate the fact that women on Lesvos were free to express their opinions and feelings not only within the structure of the community, but in philosophy and poetry as well. The Syracusans set up a statue of her, and in Lesvos coins were struck bearing her face and the inscription: Sappho of Lesvos. Alcaeus was the originator of a meter that bears his name. He placed his satirical wit at the service of the aristocracy and flayed the democrats with his sarcasm. At the same time he distinguished himself in virtually all forms of lyric poetry. His verses are dominated by eroticism, the vehemence of his political feelings, and aggressiveness. He was violently hostile to Pittacus. When the people of Mytilene put an end to the civil unrest which had plagued the town and elected Pittacus ruler, Alcaeus was exiled. He later received an amnesty and returned to his native island. Sappho and Alcaeus are depicted together on a large number of coins. Intellectual life on Lesvos was also of importance during the Byzantine period. Under the Turks, however, the island was intellectually dead. Its only center of culture was at the Leimonos Monastery which was built in 1523 by the then Metropolitan St. Ignatius Agalanos. Scholarly clerics were active on the island and beyond and carried on the cultural tradition. During the years leading up to the Greek Revolution of 1821 quite a number of Metropolitans were distinguished for their reform activities. Benjamin of Lesvos was one of the most important and appealing figures and was given the title "Teacher to the Nation." He also studied on a scholarship in Pisa and Paris where his subjects included Mathematics, Physics, Astronomy and Philosophy. Benjamin was one of the first to introduce modern philosophy and the physical sciences to Greece. The new system of education which he implemented was based on the spirit of the European Enlightenment. Intellectual life flourished on the island, particularly in the years immediately following the achievement of Greek independence, with writers such as Stratis Myrivilis and Ilias Venezis to name only two. Today a galaxy of writers carry on this blossoming of the arts that occurred in the period between the wars and has brought honor to the island. The most outstanding of them is the Nobel laureate Odysseas Elytis, whose roots lie in the heart of Lesvos, near the picturesque Bay of Yera. The following lines from the poem "Axion Esti" are characteristic:

For a moment I thought that I had seen
The one who gave his blood that I be healed
Climbing his rough and holy way
for yet another time.

Once more to rest upon the waters of Yera
all five fingers taking light on their own
Papados, Plakados, Palaiokipos
Skopelos, Mesagros
Authority and portion of my generation.

Lesvos is also the native island of the great painter Georgios Iakovidis, and the distinguished Paris art critic Stratis Eleftheriadis-Teriad, who vigorously promoted the folk painter Theophilos, and who will receive more extensive mention further down. At present the intellectual and artistic tradition is carried on in a variety of exciting forms.

Folk Art

*Since ancient times the people of Lesvos
have been involved with the arts. Finds which
have come to light at different times, and
particularly in the excavations carried out at
ancient Thermi, provide evidence that at the
beginning of the 14th century B.C. Mycenean
clay vessels and bronze swords of the
Mycenean and Cretan type were imported to the
island and used as models by its inhabitants.
It was under this outside influence that ceramics
and the art of working in bronze developed.
The black vessels of Lesvos were much sought
after abroad and brought considerable profits
to the island's potters. The art of pottery today,
thousands of years later, still finds its most
admirable morphological and decorative
expression in the town of Ayiassos where its
practice has been carried on without interruption
up to the present. The means employed are still
traditional ones: clay, potter's wheels and ovens,
but the results are a testament to the skill of the
potter's hands, and the decorative composition
of the ceramics is derived from
the inspiration and artistic sense of the folk
craftsman. Great strides have been made in
wood-carving on Lesvos over the centuries.
The intricate carved wooden iconostases which
adorn the churches in the towns and countryside
are particularly fine. The wooden chests of
Lesvos, which used to be decorated by the old
craftsmen with carved designs and Byzantine
double-headed eagles, are much sought after.
Olive wood, which is plentiful on the island,
provides the islanders with the raw material
to express their innate artistic bent. In imitations
of ancient vessels, as well as in giving shape
to their own inspirations, the craftsmen produce
amphoras and a wide range of other items using
the lathe and various other tools of the wood
carver's art. Many of these items are decorated
with artistic designs done by the makers
themselves. Working in olive wood is a craft
that flourishes in the town of Mytilene.
The working of semi-precious stones and the
production of silverware are also of importance
on the island.*

The Architecture of Lesvos

The Turkish invasion, the passage of time, and the recent introduction of the use of concrete, have all inevitably caused appalling losses and changes to the beautiful town of Mytilene. In the time of the Turkish occupation the houses in Mytilene and the villages were designed to answer to the climatic conditions and the rudimentary needs of the inhabitants.

Unlike these town and country houses were the "towers" which were built within large, enclosed areas and which, as 18th century travellers report, were to be found only in the environs of Mytilene itself. To construct a house of more than one storey, the old builders of Lesvos made a framework of chestnut wood with iron supports at the ends done in such a way that the walls were held together and the whole structure bound into one anti-seismic unit. Later the picturesque wooden balconies ("sachnisia") with their fretted railings and other decorations made their appearance. Characteristic of the houses of the leading families are the Ionic and Doric pillars, peristyles, pediments, memorial facades and niches. The ceilings in the reception rooms and the corridors are decorated with mythical scenes.

Several mansions can still be found today. The Alepoudellis (Elytis) and the Papadopoulos mansions have been kept in excellent condition. The dozens of "towers" which can still be seen in the suburbs, are notable for their stone construction, their height, their sturdy doors, the small fanlights in the lower part and the projecting balcony to give more room on the upper floor, with its windows set at right angles. They have the general appearance of a stronghold. A basic characteristic of almost all the settlements on Lesvos is their "urban" nature. In many places one still finds the rowhouse system and courtyards are entirely absent. In the cases where there are courtyards they are surrounded by high walls and completely cut off from the street.

Mansions in Lesvos
which are still kept in excellent repair.

Ceilings decorated with mythological depictions from the mansions of Lesvos.

MUSEUMS

The Archaeological Museum

In a traditional mansion on the outer harbor, one can see, arranged in cases, characteristic examples of prehistoric ceramics and clay idols from the settlement at Thermi, dating from the Early Bronze Age as well as Geometric and Archaic vessels from Antissa, terracottas from ancient Pyrra, vessels from the Classical and Hellenistic periods and gold coins from the area of Messoi. Some Aeolian capitals may be seen preserved under glass covers in the courtyard; they are from the temple of Apollo at Klopedi (6th century B.C.). Also on display are the marble throne of the orator Potamon, small sacrificial altars and other objects.

The archaeological wealth of Lesvos is housed in the basements of the mansion and consists of a multitude of finds, dating to the middle of the fourth millennium B.C. A new archaeological museum has been created in the area of Kioski, Mytilene, with lavish exhibits that stretch from the Archaic to the Roman period.

1. *Entrance to museum.*
2. *Octagon with Orpheus,*
   a mosaic from the Menander House.
3. *Column capital from the museum's courtyard.*
4. *Mosaic from the new museum.*

The Byzantine Ecclesiastical Museum

This museum is located opposite St. Therapon and contains all the island's notable icons which are not in daily use, and all the other items that faith and artistic talent have created to express the purity of Christian feeling, representative of the items which have been used in the course of Christian worship. The museum also has on display vestments embroidered with pearls, sections of fine iconostases from old churches, and valuable church relics as well as manuscripts and old religious books. Superb Roman mosaics lie under the Byzantine Ecclesiastical Museum.

Icons from the Byzantine Museum.
1. St. John the Divine (15th century).
2. The Virgin Mary, the Unfading Rose (1796).

1

2

The Old Lesvos House

The old Lesvos house, which disappeared after being defeated by modern culture and the contemporary demands of the average householder, has been "recreated", in breathtaking and complete detail, by the Women's Society of Lesvos, bringing back to life the type of house prevalent from 1800-1900 with all of its attractive and quaint furnishings. Thus, in an old mansion near the Cathedral Church, a complete domestic scene from Lesvos of the past century has been created which thrills the viewer with its wealth of objects and charms you by reminding you of how calm and sweet the atmosphere was which for centuries lent beauty to the life of the inhabitants during difficult periods.

The Folk Art Museum

On the waterfront, next to the local bus terminal, the Folk Art Museum is housed in the former Harbor-Master's building, which was recently renovated. This museum contains a wide variety of exhibits from different periods which exemplify the island's popular art and illustrate its past. There are clay pots, old water jugs from Ayiassos and Mantamados, and plates painted with scenes from everyday life as it was lived in the past, and much, much more.

Interior of the old Lesvos house.

The Teriad Museum and Library

The Teriad Museum and Library was founded in 1972, next to the Theophilos Museum in Vareia. It is a large building with specially designed spaces. It stands in the same enormous olive grove as the art well-known critic's family house, and the area has been designated as a place of outstanding beauty. Sixteen of the twenty rooms have been set aside for a permanent exhibition of Teriad's 29 books. There is a complete copy of each, numbered and signed, in a special case, plus a number of single pages framed on the walls to give the visitor an idea of the contents of the books.

Among the exhibits are five books illustrated by Chagall: Gogol's "Dead Souls", the Bible, La Fontaine's "Fables", "The Circus", with texts by the artist, and Longus' "Daphnis and Chloe". There are three books with Greek themes: Theocritus' "Idylls", and "Lucius and the Ass" and the "Dialogues " of Lucian, illustrated with novel woodcuts by Henri Lauren. In addition there are Hesiod's "Works and Days", illustrated by Jacques Villon, Pierre Reverdy's "Song of the Dead", illustrated by Picasso, Fernand Leger's "The Circus", Le Corbusier's "Poem of the Right Angle", Matisse's "Jazz" and "Paris without End" with a text and fifty lithographs by the great sculptor and close friend of Teriad, Giacometti. The other rooms contain some issues of Teriad's magazines "Minotaure" and "Verve", while three rooms on the ground floor contain forty paintings by Theophilos. These are the paintings that Teriad arranged to be shown at the Louvre and which made the great folk artist world-famous. Another area of the museum contains paintings by the great Yannis Tsarouchis, a friend of Teriad. The Vareia-Akrotiri area, in which the museums are located, is 4 km. from the town of Mytilene.

The Theophilos Museum

This building has five rooms and houses 86 works by the Lesvos folk painter. It was built in 1965 at Vareia at the expense of the internationally renowned art critic and publisher, Stratis Eleftheriadis-Teriad. Theophilos, who was called "Tsolias", "Evzone", because he always wore Greek national dress, was born at Vareia in 1873 and died in 1934, after a life of deprivation and poverty. His works are primitive in their conception of anatomy and perspective, but owe much of their charm to special substances used in the preparation of the paints which give them stability and a glossy texture. Theophilos painted in houses, churches and cafes, and often without pay, wherever he could get a plate of food or even just a glass of wine or ouzo. A man of spontaneity, he was most drawn to themes taken from nature and history.

Teriad met him in 1928 and was immediately impressed by his primitive grasp of artistic essentials and the harmony displayed by his works. He asked Theophilos to paint on canvas (previously he had painted on wood or done murals), in an attempt to save for posterity some of the freshness and truth of the artist's work. According to Teriad, Theophilos never asked him for money. Thus, the "Tsolias" entered a new creative period at the end of his life and produced some 120 works which are regarded as his most representative. This period is notable for the use of softer colors and a more "artistic" line. It is due solely to Teriad that Theophilos became an established name, with works on display even in the Louvre. The humble vagabond did not live to enjoy his fame, but he must have appreciated the respect and attention shown to him by a man from the world of art, in contrast to the mockery of ordinary people.

Some of the most famous works in the museum are those showing the Limnian Shepherd, the Bay of Yera, and the Fisherman's Dance, to name but a few.

Works of Theophilos at the Vareia museum.

MYTILENE

Mytilene is the capital of Lesvos, and its name has for many years also been used for the island as a whole, at least in Greek. It is 188 nautical miles from Piraeus and has 25,000 inhabitants. The town is built on seven hills and its main sections are "Kioski", the center with its older buildings, and the western part which runs out into the ever growing suburbs with their low, picturesque houses. Kioski is the old aristocratic neighborhood, near the Venetian castle, and in ancient times was isolated from the remainder of the town by a canal which had quite a lot of bridges along it. This canal, which joined the north and south harbors, was gradually built over, thus uniting the two parts of the town.

The district still contains mansions which are fine examples of the traditional style of architecture. The main artery which traverses Kioski ends at the north harbor which is no longer in use. The broken up jetty and other ruins from the past can still be seen. This is the area of Epano Skala. Various Turkish buildings still exist there such as the Geni Mosque, a building from 1823-1828, which also had characteristic Greek architectural elements, the old Turkish baths and a ruined minaret. A short distance from the harbor ancient ruins have been found and the mouth of canal, which during antiquity divided Mytilene into two parts and made a small island out of the whole complex where the castle is.

At various parts of this northern section of Mytilene important ruins of ancient and Roman buildings have been brought to light. Of these the Menander House and the Ancient Theater are of exceptional importance (see pages 59-60).

Aerial photograph of Mytilene.

the town - the castle - south of the town

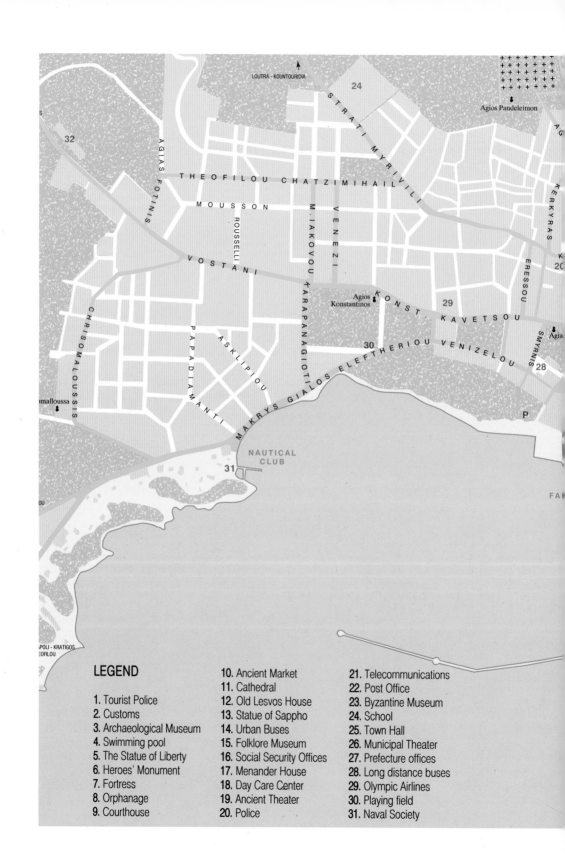

LEGEND

1. Tourist Police
2. Customs
3. Archaeological Museum
4. Swimming pool
5. The Statue of Liberty
6. Heroes' Monument
7. Fortress
8. Orphanage
9. Courthouse
10. Ancient Market
11. Cathedral
12. Old Lesvos House
13. Statue of Sappho
14. Urban Buses
15. Folklore Museum
16. Social Security Offices
17. Menander House
18. Day Care Center
19. Ancient Theater
20. Police
21. Telecommunications
22. Post Office
23. Byzantine Museum
24. School
25. Town Hall
26. Municipal Theater
27. Prefecture offices
28. Long distance buses
29. Olympic Airlines
30. Playing field
31. Naval Society

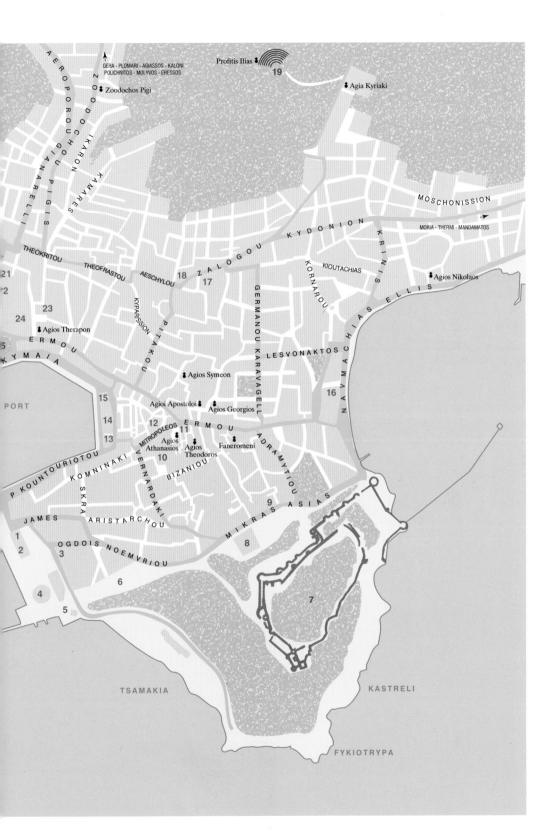

GERA - PLOMARI - AGIASSOS - KALONI
POLICHNITOS - MOLYVOS - ERESSOS

Zoodochos Pigi

Profitis Ilias

19

Agia Kyriaki

MOSCHONISSION

MORIA - THERMI - MANDAMATOS

AEROPOROU
PIGIS
PANARELLI
IKARON
KAMARES
ZOODOCHOS

THEOKRITOU
THEOFRASTOU
AESCHYLOU
18 ZALOGOU KYDONION
17
KORNAROU
KIOUTACHIAS
KRINIS
Agios Nikolaos

21
*2
23
24
Agios Therapon
ERMOU
KYMAIA
KYPARISSION
PITAKOU
GERMANOU KARAVAGELI
LESVONAKTOS
NAVMACHIAS ELLIS

PORT

15
14
13
Agios Symeon
Agioi Apostoloi
Agios Georgios
16

12
11
ERMOU
Agios
Athanasios
Agios
Theodoros
Faneromeni
ADRAMYTIOU

MITROPOLEOS
10
BIZANIOU
P KOUNTOURIOTOU
KOMNINAKI
VERNARDAKI
SKRA
ARISTARCHOU
JAMES
9
MIKRAS ASIAS

1
2
3
OGDOIS NOEMVRIOU
8

4
6
7

5

TSAMAKIA
KASTRELI

FYKIOTRYPA

Statue of Liberty - Cathedral

Starting off from the Customs House you will reach the old mansion which houses the Archaeological Service and then arrive at the Statue of Liberty. This is a bronze copy of the more famous statue in New York, and is based on a design by Georgios Iakovidis, a great painter from the island.

On an extension of the waterfront street is the National Tourist Organization's beach at Apeli which is small and clean and near it, on a small rise in the pine grove, is a rather peculiar bust to Sappho created by the American artist Henrietta Forsch and presented to the town of Mytilene. The area is impressive for its sheer and rocky coast line, particularly "Fikiotrypa" ("Seaweed-hole") a rock with a strange shape which was used by the German occupation forces as a lookout post.

At Epano Skala, on the site of "Kourtzi", low down, next to the sea, was found a large necropolis from the 4th and 3rd centuries B.C. In the same area, close to the mouth of the ancient canal, have been found the ruins of a temple and remains of a "house of Lesvos". The foundations of massive walls recently came to light during construction near the Masonic Lodge. The northern part of the Mytilene contains the imposing Cathedral and the Metropolitan Megaron. The church was built at the end of the 16th and beginning of the 17th century and is a triple-aisled cruciform basilica dedicated to the the Sts. Athanasius and Cyril. The altar is one of the finest pieces of post-Byzantine wood-carving to be found.

The bell-tower at the entrance to the church is made of stone from Sarmousak and is in the Gothic style, in contrast to the church viewed as a whole.

1

4

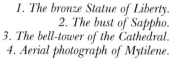

1. *The bronze Statue of Liberty.*
2. *The bust of Sappho.*
3. *The bell-tower of the Cathedral.*
4. *Aerial photograph of Mytilene.*

Waterfront - Market

Behind the Cathedral important remains of an ancient semicircular building have been found, and these are open to the public. The lavish construction of the building, its altar of tightly coiled grooves and its statue-bases, plus its location in the heart of the town near the canal which linked the north and south harbors, have led archaeologists to conclude that this must have been part of the ancient market (Agora). The center of the town extends from the harbor to the ruins of the Turkish aqueduct, the arches of which can be seen from quite a distance as one enters the port.

The waterfront and the market street running parallel to it are where the pulse of Mytilenian life beats. The waterfront is the site of most of the banks, travel agencies, pastry shops, restaurants, photographers' studios and folk art shops, while grocer's shops, pharmacies, florists and booksellers may be found on the market street.

Ayios Therapon

A short distance from the quay is the imposing church of **Ayios Therapon** (St. Therapon), which is reputed to stand on the site of the ancient Asclepieion. Building began in 1860. Architecturally it is very impressive. It is a triple-aisled basilica with neoclassical elements and influences from the Renaissance. The church possesses some fine icons. Opposite this church is the Byzantine Ecclesiastical Museum. Nearby, right in the heart of the town, you will find the municipal park, the Municipal Theater as well as the neoclassical Boys' High School. Near the Prefecture offices is the long distance bus station with the park of St. Irene and a chapel of the same name. Next to the park is Square of Cypriot Patriots and to the west of that the Post Office (ELTA), the Agricultural Bank and the Telephone Company (OTE). When the latter was to be built impressive classical buildings were found when the foundation were being dug.

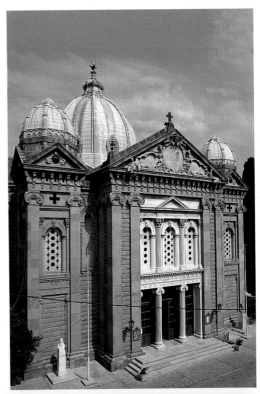

The majestic church of Ayios Therapon.

*Panoramic view of the town of Mytilene
from its Castle.*

The Castle

Directly above the pine woods, which is one of the true beauties of the town, stands the castle. It is one of the largest in the Mediterranean, but a good deal of it has, with the passage of time, fallen down or been otherwise damaged. Some restoration and shoring up have been carried out in recent years. It cannot all be assigned to any particular period, but the oldest parts probably date from the time of Justinian. Ancient materials were used in the building as can be seen from an inspection of the walls, and these would lead to the conclusion that there was an ancient garrison there too.

The first official mention of the castle is in a Venetian registry of 1260. It was renovated by Francesco Gattelusi in 1373, and added to during the Turkish occupation. It was during that period that the Turkish seminary was built within its walls. That building still survives.

The Gattelusi palace was also inside the castle and it is still standing, almost complete. It is locally known as the "Queen's Tower". A plaque with well-preserved reliefs can be seen built into the wall of the Queen's Tower. There is an eagle on one side, and the horseshoes of the Gattelusi arms on the other, with four Bs, while representations of Roman gladiators frame the whole design.

The arms of the Palaeologos family can be seen over the outer gate a double-headed eagle with two Bs and a single eagle. Other plaques can be found at other points of the castle.

The castle is honeycombed with tunnels which were used as shelters for women and children during battles.

1. 2. Views from the castle
3. Interior of the chapel to the Panayia 3

The specially designed openings which were built to allow light and air to enter the tunnels can still be seen today. These tunnels run out under the town, and local tradition has it that a secret exit exists but none has yet been discovered. The tradition goes on to say that one of the tunnels contains statues of inestimable artistic value. Inside the castle it is also worth paying a visit to the Roman, or Byzantine, cistern, which is made of special materials resistant to leakage and is still in marvelous condition. It was constructed to catch rainwater.

The castle experienced three main building stages: Byzantine, Genoese and Turkish. The ancient materials used were treated with respect, as can be seen from the prominent positions in which they were placed in the walls. During the time of the Gattelusi the castle was considered one of the strongest in the East and almost impossible to conquer. Even after all the looting and destruction it has suffered, the walls are still a marvellous example of medieval military engineering.

The Menander House

In the Chorafa neighborhood, about 500 m. from the ancient theater, have been found the remains of a house with marvellous mosaic floors depicting scenes from the comedies of Menander, along with other motifs typical of the 3rd and 4th centuries A.D. This edifice is known as "The Menander House". The most outstanding of the mosaics is the so-called "Orpheus Octagon". Orpheus is shown in the center of an octagonal frame playing his lyre with animals and birds below him. It would appear that the mosaics were the work of a folk craftsman, but they are nonetheless notable for their perfection of expression and the subtlety of their color combinations.

The mosaics from the Menander House have been transferred to the Archaeological Museum of Mytilene.

The Ancient Theater

The ancient theater is set in a hollow dug into a hillside covered with a small pine forest, a short distance from the end of the uphill road which leads to the church of Ayia Kyriaki. Its location there at the highest point of the town appears to have constituted the aesthetic high point of a wider monumental beautification of the area. Excavations carried out in 1958 by the archaeologist D. Evangelidis brought to light the orchestra and parts of the stage and the hollow of the theater. Evangelidis claims that the theater was among the largest in Greece, with seats for 15,000 spectators, which places it on the same scale as the theater at Epidaurus. It dates from the Hellenistic period and it was renovated by the Romans during a period when the island was flourishing culturally. The excavations uncovered the ruins of an altar dedicated to the priestess Potamille, and a fragmented and headless marble statue of the priestess, inscriptions, an arm of a more than life-size statue, and a drainage system employing clay pipes.

None of the stone seats were in their original positions, and in earlier periods many had been used for the construction of various buildings, and particularly the renovation of the castle by the Gattelusi. The acoustics of the theater were excellent, and visitors can still prove this to themselves today. Pompey was so impressed by the theater on his visit to the island that he ordered a similar one to be built in Rome. Thus the theater of Lesvos served as a model for the famous Pompeian theater in the Roman capital. The lower kerkides (rows of seats) were known as the "proedrial" ("presidential") seats and were reserved for dignitaries.

A track about 150 m. long, passable by car, leads the visitor to the gate. To the west of the ancient theater, near the Ayia Kyriaki graveyard, are a few remains of the ancient polygonal walls of the town.

The ancient theater, at the highest point of the town.

SOUTH OF THE TOWN

South of the center of the town is **Makriyalos** (literally, "long beach") the most picturesque side of Mytilene. All along the road there are marvellous buildings, and the whole area, with the installations of the Naval Club to the rear, retains something of its old charm. In the cool suburb of **Halikes** (Lower, Middle and Upper), is the Metropolitan's residence. This is an impressive building with a fine chapel inside, the walls and the roof of which are decorated with paintings of saints from the island, done in the Byzantine style, designed by the famous writer and painter Fotis Kontoglou and executed by his pupils. The view of Mytilene from the Metropolitan's residence and Halikes in general is superb. Above the Naval Club is the most ancient Christian monument on the island. It consists of a cruciform chamber carved out of the rock, of the type in which Christian martyrs were often buried when religious persecution was at its height. **Monopetro**, on the other side of this rise, has a quiet beach where the atmosphere, especially on summer afternoons, can become strange and dreamy.

Sourada - Akleidiou

The southern suburbs of Mytilene are famed for their beauty, tranquillity and mansions. The suburbs of **Sourada** and **Akleidiou**, are to be found on an extension of the Makriyialos road with its lush vegetation and characteristic towers. These charming edifices stand in large gardens full of trees, which only add to their charm. The mansions on the left hand side of the road show how much care and attention the rich people of the town bestowed on their houses in former times, and the skill of the craftsmen and architects of the period with a strong foreign influence. The Fotiades house is worthy of note as a classic example of the architecture of the island.

You come to a church to the Panayia (Virgin Mary), set high up among the trees in the brilliant light rather like a painting done by an artist who had a profound feeling for harmony. The view from the churchyard over the town and the sea is limitless and evocative. It has been suggested that Sappho wrote some of her poems on this spot and it was certainly the place to which the French poetess Rene Vivien (1877-190) came in her melancholy to contemplate perfect beauty and the magic of Sapphic verse.

Impressive mansions on a street in Sourada.

Panoramic view of Vareia.

Vareia - Akrotiri - Kratigos

In the the suburbs of **Vareia**, **Akrotiri** and **Kratigos**, you will find beaches for swimming, especially the one known as "Vigla", which attracts a lot of people in summer. At Akrotiri there are a number of old houses typical of local architecture. This is the spot at which the wealthy spent their summers during the Gattelusi period, when the area was renowned for its healthy climate. Here is where the Theophilos Museum and the Museum of Modern Art are located (see page 46).

Pligoni - Taxiarches - Ayia Marina

Amid the heavy vegetation on the eastern slopes of Amali are **Pligoni**, **Taxiarchs** and **Ayia Marina**, with wonderful views out over the sea. The church of the Taxiarchs ("Archangels") is a masterpiece of church architecture. Near the village is the cave of St. Bartholomew, the largest on the island, and full of stalactites. After 6 kilometers you reach **Neapoli**. Here there are rooms for rent and seaside restaurants. At 8 km. you reach the airport in the Kratigos district.

Ayios Ermoyenis - Koundouridia

After 23 km. you come to Ayios Ermoyenis, a romantic little beach with a chapel of the same name set among pine trees and thick undergrowth. There is a turn-off here from the public road to **Loutra**, a village standing among vast expanses of olive trees. Various scattered ancient ruins have been found near here and there are some Byzantine remains to be seen as well. About three kilometers to the southeast of the village are the ruins of an Early Christian basilica. Excavations have brought to light a colorful mosaic from the main aisle of the church, which is now covered by a roof to protect it from the weather.

Koundouridia is the port serving the area. Small boats ply the mouth of the Gulf of Yera to **Perama** on the other side (see page 76), which during the summer is a center for the commercial and social life of all the inhabitants of the villages of Yera. In the bay about three hundred meters from Koundouridia to the right, lies the tiny island of **Ayios Isidoros**, with a chapel and the remains of what are probably Byzantine fortifications. Boats are available for hire, and pleasant trips may be taken into the bay and along the coastline, especially at sunset or on quiet nights.

1. The village of Taxiarchs, Mytilene to the rear.
2. The beach at Ayios Ermoyenis.

6

EASTERN LESVOS
Thermi - Mantamados - Sykamnia

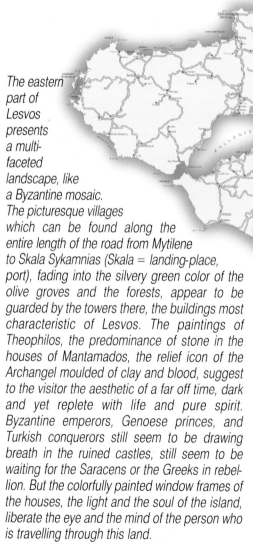

The eastern part of Lesvos presents a multi-faceted landscape, like a Byzantine mosaic. The picturesque villages which can be found along the entire length of the road from Mytilene to Skala Sykamnias (Skala = landing-place, port), fading into the silvery green color of the olive groves and the forests, appear to be guarded by the towers there, the buildings most characteristic of Lesvos. The paintings of Theophilos, the predominance of stone in the houses of Mantamados, the relief icon of the Archangel moulded of clay and blood, suggest to the visitor the aesthetic of a far off time, dark and yet replete with life and pure spirit. Byzantine emperors, Genoese princes, and Turkish conquerors still seem to be drawing breath in the ruined castles, still seem to be waiting for the Saracens or the Greeks in rebellion. But the colorfully painted window frames of the houses, the light and the soul of the island, liberate the eye and the mind of the person who is travelling through this land.

The view of the coast of Asia Minor, with all its echoes of ancient Greece, the place for which the Greeks fought so many nations, starting from the time of the Trojan War, inevitably draws each visitor into the world of myth that he or she will only be able to experience here, myths that are linked to each other in a unique way, such as the Christian faith and ancient tradition and mythology in the singular church of Panayia Gorgona (Virgin Mary the Mermaid) at Skala Sykamnias. Today the eastern coast of Lesvos is buzzing with life. Here the development of tourism includes the famed therapeutic springs at Thermi as well as the ancient and more recent monuments scattered throughout the area. This eastern coast of Lesvos, so full of lovely landscapes and memories embodied in noteworthy sites, is what we will be touring in this chapter.

Moria - Roman Aqueduct

Leaving Mytilene, you turn off the main road after 6 km. and go to **Moria**, a village with picturesque towers, amid olive groves and orchard-gardens. At the entrance to the village is the church of Ayios Vasileios (St. Basil) from the 17th century with an artistically crafted carved wooden iconostasis and a number of icons among which is the "Panayia ton Asmaton" ("The Virgin Mary of Songs") done by a priest at the church. A short distance from the village are the ruins of several arches from a **Roman aqueduct**, the so-called "Kamares" which was built of the grey marble of Lesvos. The visitor reaches the site by following a lovely stone-paved road that starts at the village. In antiquity the aqueduct supplied Mytilene with water from the district of Ayiassos, approximately 26 km. away. There is also an ancient quarry in the district, from the 4th century B.C. the marble of which was used for, among other things, the building of the seats of the ancient theater of Mytilene. Finally, in the environs of Outza there is a cave with openings in the ceiling which let in sufficient light.

Panayiouda - Pyrgoi Thermis - Thermi

Continuing on toward the north you reach **Panayiouda** (6 km.) a coastal settlement with tavernas and restaurants on the sea which attracts many sun-bathers and holiday-makers during the summer period. To the left, on top of a hill choked with greenery, you see Afalonas where there is also a church to the Panayia (Virgin Mary) with an artistic iconostasis while a little further north is Pamfila with Paralia on the sea, an especially picturesque village. It has towers subject to preservation, such as those of Chatzisavvas and Saltas, monuments to this special form of local architecture. The imposing church of Ayia Varvara (St. Barbara) in the middle of the village is of exceptional interest with its marble iconostasis in relief, a work of the famous Tinian sculptor Yiannoulis Chalepas. The next settlement you reach, 10 km. from the town, is **Pyrgoi Thermis** which owes its name to the approximately 160 towers in the area (pyrgos=tower).

Above: The arches of the Roman aqueduct.
Below: The seaside settlement of Panayiouda.

Outside the village is the church of Panayia Trouloti ("The Virgin Mary of the Dome") the second oldest Christian monument on Lesvos after the Ypsilou Monastery. It is dated to the 14th century and houses the renowned icon of the Virgin Mary and Infant, an icon that was built into the iconostasis probably while the church itself was being constructed because the icon is believed to be two centuries older. The visitor must also visit the private church of the Panayia Faneromeni ("The Virgin Mary Revealed") in the courtyard of the renovated Taktikos tower. In this building drawings by Theophilos were found, probably from his early period. Archaeological excavations carried out in 1930-1932 in the coastal area of the village brought to light an important settlement from the Minoan and Mycenean period; at the end of the excavations it was covered up again. At Paralia Thermis (paralia=beach) were found the ruins of a temple to Thermia Artemis as well as medieval and more recent ruins of baths and related installations. The finds from the excavations are on exhibit at the Archaeological Museum of Mytilene.

There is also a renovated mill at Paralia that one can visit and there is a marvelous beach at Kanoni, near the main road.

Thermi, the main settlement in the area (12 km.), is a tourist center with a complete infrastructure which attracts visitors from throughout the world, because of its important therapeutic springs but also because of its beauty. It has a number of towers, only two of which have been kept in good condition: those of Magnisalis and Tsoukaladelis. Near the road is the church of Ayia Thekla in the courtyard of which is an ancient circular altar, a moving example of coexistence and continuity. Near the entrance to the town there is a rock with a number of peculiar carvings on it called "Tis Grias ton Serai" ("The Old Woman's Seraglio"). North of Thermi is the district of Ai-Giorgis (St. George) with country chapel of the same name nestled in pine woods, and the equally beautiful area of Ayia Akindyna with a sand beach at Petalidi. There is also a road from Thermi to the mountainous villages of Pigi and Komi, about 8 km. to the west.

The Ayios Raphael Monastery on the Karyes elevation.

Ayios Raphael Monastery

West of Thermi, 3 km. into the interior of the island, is the convent of Ayios Raphael, on the elevation of Karyes where it is said the Karyes Monastery once stood, before it was destroyed by the Saracens in 1453. That monastery was built on the foundations of the earlier one by the monks Raphael, Nikolaos and Rouviem who died as martyrs at the hands of the Turks. Since then Raphael has been worshipped as a saint and is thought to work miracles. The present buildings play host to many pilgrims with guest-houses and the restaurants. Finally, the church of Ayia Magdalini (Mary Magdalene) is located in the convent's enclosure.

*Leaving the monastery and Thermi behind in the olive groves and with a view of the shores of Asia Minor, you reach **Mystegna** and **Nees Kydonies**, beautiful settlements set on a tranquil, rocky coast whose shops and beaches attract many holidaymakers in summer, the principal beach being at Xambelia. Nearing Mantamados, you can visit in the area of Ayios Stephanos a church of the same name set deep within the trees and considered to be one of the most noteworthy Christian monuments on Lesvos. In the neighboring district of Aspro-potamos there is a lovely beach.*

Mantamados - Taxiarch Church

***Mantamados** (36 km.) impresses all those who see its architecture for the first time. Built of stone and with tile roofs, its colors once protected it from a pirates but today make for a dynamic and imposing image. Mantamados is famed for its **Church of the Taxiarch** (Archangel Michael), the patron saint of the island, as well as for the monastery of the same name which lies just outside the town amid olive and pine trees. The famed icon of the Archangel found in the church is a rare Orthodox icon in relief, made of an unknown material. Legend says that in the period that followed Byzantium there was a monastery in the area. During one of the Saracen attacks, the pirates slaughtered the monks except for one who managed to crawl up on the roof. The pirates went after him but every time they tried to seize him a storm-tossed sea opened before their feet. After abandoning their hunt for the monk and fleeing in fear, the monk, attributing his salvation to a miracle of the Archangel, obviously the saint honored at the old monastery, took clay, mixed it with the blood of his fellow monks who had been killed and created the icon of the saint that has survived down to our time*

The monastery houses many important relics among, which is the prelate's tunicle of the Ecumenical Patriarch Gregory V: this national martyr was hung by the Turks in Constantinople. The feast-day of the Taxiarch, the patron saint of Lesvos, is held on the "Sunday of the Magi" (the Sunday nearest Epiphany) amid great pomp and with thousands of pilgrims present from throughout the Christian world.

The miracle-working icon of Ayios Taxiarchis.

Ancient customs have survived in this festival, which has been adopted by Orthodox tradition, such as animal sacrifice. On the Friday before the feast, a bull is decked out in gold and other objects and flowers and is then slaughtered so its meat can be made into the "keskesi" stew, and cooked for the entire night in large cauldrons set up outside. All through the night people there sing and dance while on Saturday there are horse races, the trophy consisting of a wreath and money. Furthermore, on the final Sunday of Carnival there is a reenactment of the traditional way of fishing with nets along the beach. In Mantamados there is also found the church of Ayios Vasileios (St. Basil); its carved wooden iconostasis has depictions of various subjects. Moreover, there is an exceptional example of industrial architecture of the 19th century which is a renovated olive press that today serves as a cultural center. Finally, in the area of Sarakina are the ruins of a Byzantine castle while at Palios, to the east, ancient carved tombs have been found.

Sykamnia - Skala Sykamnias

Continuing on toward Sykamnia, you will first reach Kapi, set among olive groves, a picturesque village, with its seaside settlement at **Limanio**, which is suitable for tranquil holidays. A secondary road sets off from Kapi going to **Pelopi** and **Ypsilometopos,** a village whose church, the Taxiarchs (Archangels), has a carved wooden and gilt iconostasis while the area is also noted for the ruins of an Early Christian basilica dedicated to Ayia Anastasia (St. Anastasia) from the 6th century with a mosaic floor and Ionic style columns. In the area near Kapi and, more specifically, at Palaiokastro, are the ruins of a medieval fortification. After Kapi comes **Kleiou** whose port is at the lovely beach in the area of **Tsonia**. Nearing the end of the excursion you reach **Sykamnia** (46 km.) built on the slopes of Mt. Lepetymnos, covered with pine woods and plane trees. Its characteristic street lay-out and its stone houses, the mansions with the "sachnisia" (a kind of enclosed wooden balcony), the inscriptions from the 19th century, and the stepped lanes, are all united into one lovely and harmonic whole. The paternal home of Stratis Myrivilis, the world-famous Greek author, is in Sykamnia, (his real name was Stratis Stamatopoulos). His house is open to visitors. A road from the village goes to Molyvos, passing through the villages of Lepetymnos and Argennos. Three kilometers to the north is **Skala Sykamnias**, a typical fishing village and the northernmost settlement on the island which faces the coast of Asia Minor. With the superb beaches surrounding it, and one of the most beautiful sunsets on the island, it is slowly becoming a summer resort. Peculiar to Sykamnia is the small church of Panayia Gorgona (The Virgin Mary Mermaid) built on a strip of land which sticks out into the sea. It took its name from a wall painting by an anonymous folk painter which depicts the Virgin Mary with a mermaid's tail in a moving amalgam of religion and folk tradition.

1. *The village of Sykamnia.*
2. 3. 4. 5. *Skala Sykamnias with the little church of "Panayia tis Gorgonas".*

The southern part of Lesvos contains two of the most important areas on the island. The Bay of Yera with its beautiful villages and its amazing natural beauty and Plomari, which was the center of the cultural and economic activity of the island for many decades. Today, the villages on Yera Bay attract a large number of tourists who come to view the picturesque straits, and experience the past in the countless monuments left there by History, both on the serene shores of the bay and in the open sea along the south coast of the island down to Plomari.

Even though tourism has given Plomari new life in the summer, it still retains the elements which once made it the center of the whole eastern Aegean, such as its industries and its distilleries which provided Lesvos with perhaps the best ouzo in Greece. This economic activity that marked the beginning of the century has left very important monuments of industrial architecture, primarily from the beginning of the 20th century, throughout southern Lesvos which complement the ancient finds, the multitude of Byzantine churches and the fortifications. The tour of south Lesvos will certainly leave the colors of the island deeply etched on the memories of the visitor: the green and silver of the riotous vegetation that covers the region, the color of the soil and the color of the rock, in part from the old factories that made Lesvos known throughout the world. But there are also the blues, the deep blue of the open Aegean sea, the gentle blue of Yera Bay and the special blue of the open sky.

LESVOS Bay of Yera - Plomari

The famous shores of the Bay of Yera.

1

2

3

4

The Bay of Yera

The Bay of Yera, for many the place that truly typifies Lesvos, is one of the most beautiful bays in the Mediterranean, verdant, with many small, picturesque settlements and with a special charm that one can only experience there. The excursion from the town of Mytilene to Plomari follows the shores of the bay for quite a distance, giving everyone the chance to enjoy the simple and pure beauty of the landscape. Leaving the town you take a short turn-off, and on the road along the coast of the Bay of Yera you reach the settlements of **Pyrgi** and **Kedros**. At the northernmost part of the bay are the Baths of Korfos, the "Therma", where there are modern therapeutic baths and a corresponding tourist infrastructure. The road that leads to Plomari and Megalochori starts at the 12th km.

1. *Perama.*
2. *The village of Papados.*
3. *Skopelos.*
4. *The site Tarti.*

Immediately after the junction, you reach the village of **Dipi**, a small, quaint harbor with fishing caiques, while in the settlement itself there are presses for olive oil and olive-pit oil. After turnoffs to the right, you reach **Mychos**, a lovely settlement in a lush green valley and then **Kato Tritos**, with the small church of the Taxiarch which has beautiful wall paintings.

The road continues on to the south, winding through the captivating landscape of the Bay of Yera and a short way after the junction with the coastal road, at **Napi**, you arrive at the tourist installations of the area. The road, however, enters the plain and from there climbs the slopes of the mountain. You will first reach **Palaiokipos**, set amid orchard-gardens and olive groves. The church of Ayios Ermolaos, built in 1795, is noteworthy. "Evriaki" on the beach is a lovely place for spending a holiday in the region. This is immediately followed by **Plakados**, an old Turkish village with abundant water and lavish gardens where the Turkish baths are still in operation; it has practically merged with **Papados** (24 km.) the main village in the area with marvellous mansions which still retains its special customs, even today, and has never lost its lively commercial activity.

The church of the Taxiarchs and the ruins of the small fortress on Kasteli are some of the other important sites in the village. In the old market can still be found the old Turkish fountain while the town's port is at Perama, along with the settlements of Marmaro and Chalatses.

The road goes just below **Mesagros** which has a ruined mosque, impressive for the coexistence of the symbols of the Cross and the Crescent Moon; one of the village bakeries has wall paintings by Theophilos with subjects connected to the cultivation of wheat and the process followed for the baking of bread, an important element of the period's folklore.

Next to it is **Skopelos**, a traditional village with the impressive church of Ayia Magdalini (St. Magdalene) beneath which are Early Christian catacombs.

The village has a beautiful square with fountains while the coastal site of **Tarti** to the south is of incomparable beauty.

Perama

Descending for the final time to the Bay of Yera, before heading south, the road arrives at Perama, Chalatses and Marmaro, settlements which administratively belong to Papados and are its ports. Perama, a resort area today, was formerly an important commercial center as evidenced by the many monuments to industrial architecture there dating from the beginning of the century. The other two settlements, and Pyrgoi as well, are fishing villages which have now been developed for tourism.

There are many small, natural harbors on the south coast of this district such as Ftelia, the harbor used by the ancient inhabitants of the area.

1. *Ayios Isidoros, with its marvellous beach.*
2. *3. Plomari.*

Ayios Isidoros - Plomari

The road now heads SW, in the direction of Plomari. You will first reach the villages of Trigonas and Plagia, while further to the north lies Milies, which is reached after you pass through **Ayios Isidoros** with its superb beach and well-developed tourist trade; you will then arrive at Plomari, 42 km. from Mytilene. At the entrance to the town is the "Tarsanades" one of the finest boatyards in the Aegean in days gone by.

The road then takes you to the famous BARBAYIANNIS distilleries and the ruins of olive presses and tanneries. **Plomari** has a special history. The town took that name in the 16th century. But the fires of 1841-1843 decimated both the "Small" and the "Large Village". On the site of the mountainous Plomari the modern day village of Megalochori was built, while present-day Plomari was erected on the coast at Potamos, on the banks of the Sedountas river. It experienced amazing growth and development

and during the opening decades of the 20th century the area was humming with life from trade generated by the distilleries, the tanneries, the olive oil plants and dozens of other factories. Today it still has the most important ouzo distilleries in the country and every year there is heavy tourist traffic, particularly in the area of Ayios Isidoros. The harbor is protected by a large breakwater and is full of fishing boats. Near the sea is a park with palm trees and behind it superb buildings from the beginning of the 20th century, such as the traditional coffee house called "Athanasiadeio" and the building housing the Cultural Society, named "Benjamin o Lesbios" ("Benjamin of Lesvos"). In front of the important Folklore Museum runs the street which houses the market of Plomari while behind it is the old pharmacy of Logoumidis. At right about that point a stone-paved street heads in the direction of a quaint little bridge over the river and a large plane tree in the middle of the square along with the church of Ayios Nikolaos.

2

3

On the banks of the river can be found many old mansions still retaining all their multi-colored and impressive characteristics and throughout the town marble Turkish fountains can still be encountered. The building that houses the town's High School and Lyceum is also lovely while the old soap factory, which has been renovated, is of considerable interest, having been turned into an ultra-modern cultural center. There are other noteworthy churches in the town, such as Ayia Paraskevi, with its marble iconostasis and **Profitis Ilias** (Prophet Elijah) at the highest point of the town. Approximately ten kilometers higher up is Megalochori, set in a dense forest, the "Switzerland of Lesvos", as it is called. Its important sites include the mansion of "Benjamin of Lesvos". The area of Plomari is full of small settlements and sites, the most important being Palaiochori and its port at Melinda with its lovely beach. Of special interest is the small church of Panayia tis Kryftis (The Virgin Mary of the Crypt) inside a cave.

Scenes from traditional Plomari.

8

CENTRAL LESVOS
Ayiassos - Polichnitos - Vatera

The region that extends from the pine woods of Tsamliki to the south coast of the Bay of Kalloni and Vatera on the Aegean, is a mixture of the Byzantine grandeur of the Panayia (Virgin Mary) of Ayiassos, the amazing landscapes of Karini, and history of Lesvos, all eloquently revealed by the ancient monuments in the area. The mysterious ancient towns which sank into the waters of the bay, and the legends and myths surrounding the churches and monasteries, are all imbued with the beauty of nature and the picturesqueness of the villages of central Lesvos.

That is why visitors here must be attentive, so that they will be able to discover and benefit from the beauties and the gifts of the area. Here time and the rapid pace of modern development have not been able to alter the serene, almost poetic life of the region's inhabitants. The farming and stock-raising villages, and the towers, have a humility about them closely bound to the Orthodox Church which is venerated in this area like few other areas in the country. Tourism is constantly developing, in the area of Polichnitos and Vatera, with one of the most beautiful and largest sand beaches in Europe. Ayiassos, which has devoted itself to preserving its tradition, attracts thousands of tourists each year who want to live as near as they can to the beauty of the traditional life of Lesvos in its picturesque little lanes, its Byzantine grandeur and its humble harmony. You will follow the road that goes all the way to Vatera, observing the course of history in this area which is still being written amid the beauty of its landscapes, the pure and living culture of the island.

Kerameia - Ippeios - Sykounta

On the road that goes from Mytilene to Kalloni there is a crossroads to the left leading to Ayiassos and Polichnitos at the 13th km. Passing through a plain of lush vegetation you arrive at **Kerameia**. A lovely settlement, it is of interest for the church of Ayios Georgios (St. George), built on top of ancient walls, but above all for the chapel of Ayia Sophia (Divine Wisdom) which resembles a catacomb. Continuing on you arrive, after a short drive along the main road, at **Ippeios**, famed for its fertile plain and the figs it produces. Three characteristic mansions from the period of the Turkish occupation have been preserved in the settlement, and the church of Ayios Prokopios, built in 1746, is of interest for its icons and the valuable vestments housed there. Finally, ruins from the Byzantine period can be found at Magaina. Next to Ippeios is **Sykounta**, a small village amid dense olive groves.

Asomatos - Karini

You return to the main road and along the way you reach another junction with a secondary road, this one leading to **Asomatos**, a village where weaving is still flourishing.
It is surrounded by beautiful landscapes such as Ayioi Anargyroi with its age-old trees, its beautiful gardens and the water around the small church of the same name. Proceeding along the main road again, you arrive at the enchanting site of **Karini**, one of the most beautiful natural landscapes in Lesvos.
The water of the Evergetoulas river gives life to the plane, pine, chestnut and many other trees as well, which also serve to ornament, a little further on, the site called the "Kipos tis Panayias" ("The Virgin Mary's Garden"), also of exceptional beauty. In the cafe at Karini wall paintings by Theophilos can still be seen, though half-obliterated.

View of the traditional village of Ayiassos, below Mt. Olympos.

Ayiassos

About 27 kilometers from Mytilene you reach Ayiassos, built on the NE slopes of Mt. Olymbos. Down through the ages **Ayiassos** has taken over the role of guardian of the Orthodox faith and the traditional values of the area, focused on the Panayia tin Ayiasiotissa (The Virgin Mary of Ayiassos). The village "climbs" the slopes, its main entrance being low down, to the north. The stone-paved streets and the traditional tile-roofed stone houses, with their enclosed balconies, and painted window and door frames, are held in the embrace of a dense forest consisting of pine, plane and many other trees. The church of the Panayia tis Ayiasiotissa is the dominant feature of the village and on it the life and other activities of the village are in large part focused.

1. Picturesque lane in Ayiassos.
2. The church of the Panayia Ayiasiotissa.

1

2

The "Virgin Mary and Infant", the miracle-working icon that was brought to Lesvos by Agathon the Ephesian in 803, is a work done by the Evangelist Luke, made of mastic and wax. Agathon founded a monastery in the area of Karyes, and the monks built the first church of the Panayia of Ayiassos in 1170. In 1814 the present magnificent church was built, a true Byzantine palace of Orthodoxy. Besides its precious icon, it houses many other relics which are on display in the Ecclesiastical Museum, while the village itself has a Folklore Museum. Ayiassos also boasts a Cultural Center with a Library, a folklore collection and rooms for exhibitions and the showing of films.

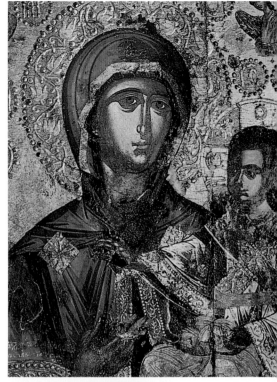

The miracle-working icon of the Virgin with Infant.

Lane in Ayiassos with folk art.

In the center of the settlement, arranged around the church, can be found the traditional cafes and commercial shops, but also new shops with tourist goods. Ayiassos also has marvellous pastries such as halva, and woven goods and wood carvings which continue to be made in the traditional manner. Finally, on Kasteli hill near the church of Ayios Evstratios and set in a pine woods, are the ruins of a fortress, probably from the Byzantine period.

Besides the large and popular celebration of the Virgin Mary's name-day on 15 August, there are also festivals held on 20 July (Prophet Elijah) and 26 October (St. Dimitrios) while the events that take place in Ayiassos during Carnival and the First Monday of Greek Lent are equally well-known and include theatrical sketches and the revival of old customs in which the local dialect plays an important part.

Ambeliko - Achladeri - Vasilika

You leave Ayiassos and continue on toward Polichnitos. On your left you will find a turn-off that leads to the mountainous settlement of **Ambeliko**, one of the oldest in modern Lesvos with documentation dating back to 1565 and many interesting churches. A few kilometers after the turn-off to Ambeliko, there is a road which leads to the beaches on the Bay of Kalloni and to **Achladeri** where ancient Pyrra is located. After that you reach **Vasilika**, at the foot of the mountains and the plain of Polichnitos framed in dense greenery. The port for these settlements is **Skala Vasilikon** where according to legend St. Paul was forced to anchor because of bad weather in 52 A.D., at a spot near the church that today bears his name. Near Skala, at the site called Kourtir, has been discovered the largest prehistoric settlement on the island, which also extends out into the sea. According to archaeologists, it is five times larger than the corresponding one at Thermi on the eastern coast of the island. A prehistoric settlement and the ruins of a Byzantine fortification have also been found in the village of Skamnoudi west of Skala.

Approaching Polichnitos, a short turn-off leads to **Lisvori**, a picturesque village with important districts around it, such as **Skala Lisvoriou** where there are the ruins of a tower with the initials of Michael Palaeologos, the site of Temenos where it said there is the oldest olive tree on the island and finally the site of Ayios Ioannis with its medicinal hot springs, the property of the community of Lisvori.

Polichnitos - Skala Polichnitou

Polichnitos lies 46 km. from Mytilene. It is a traditional and wealthy market town, formerly the main town in the region, as can be seen from its imposing mansions and neoclassical civic buildings, as well as the industrial installations from the 19th century.

Of these, the outstanding ones are those that house the schools, and the courts as well as the old renovated olive press that today is the cultural center, together with the old coffee shop next to it. Also of importance is the church of Ayios Georgios (St. George), built in 1805 on the site of an older church. The main characteristics of this large triple-aisled basilica are the carved wooden iconostasis and the three-storey bell-tower of pinkish trachyte with a clock face and a balcony on all four sides.

4 km. to the north is **Skala Polichnitou**, a fishing harbor that has developed into a tourist resort with the beaches of Skala and Nyfida, as well as dozens of shops of all kinds which operate there in the summer. Skala, still extremely picturesque today, was, as its buildings show, a highly developed commercial center with olive presses, soap factories and warehouses, and the salt-works there have supplied its inhabitants with salt since antiquity. The prehistoric settlement of Chalkies is also of interest, with the church of Ai-Yannis (St. John) and an old marble fountain (1834). In August the village celebrates the "Fourneli" festival with the traditional "casting of the nets", music, songs and much else, attracting many visitors from Skala, both locals and tourists.

Dramandriou Monastery - Vrisa

Returning to Polichnitos on the road to Vrisa and Vatera, you reach the secondary road to the **Dromandriou Monastery** from the 12th century which contains Byzantine icons and wall paintings of considerable value. Along the way you will also find the hot springs of Polichnitos, abandoned since the Turkish occupation; recently plans have been drawn up to make use of them. You continue on south through the plain until you reach **Vrisa** (50 km.) a small village surrounded by cultivated fields. On a nearby hill is a tower with a reservoir that legend says communicates with the sea via an underground passage. The churches of Zoodochos Pigi ("Life-Giving Source") with its carved wooden iconostasis and Ayios Konstantinos (St. Constantine) are of interest to the visitor.

Vatera - Ayios Phocas

At the end of the main road is **Vatera** with its famed beach, 8 km. long. This sand beach, one of the best in Europe, is a pole of attraction for vacationers, making the settlement a rapidly developing tourist resort with hotels, nightclubs, shops and all the other things a visitor might need. The area combines natural beauty with historical interest as on the headland of **Ayios Phocas**, which has a church of the same name, there were found both the ruins of ancient temple dedicated to Dionysos and an Early Christian basilica as well as various other buildings from that period. Furthermore, it is said that the area was one of the bases of operations used by the Achaeans during the Trojan War.

Vatera.

The headland of Ayios Phocas with a chapel of the same name.

Vatera, panoramic view.

According to the inhabitants of Lesvos the most beautiful areas of the island are the large pine woods called Tsamliki, and of course Molyvos, the medieval town on the north shores of the island. The forest, which extends down to the beaches on the Bay of Kalloni and stretches all the way to Ayia Paraskevi, is the pride of the inhabitants of Lesvos. However, as much as Kalloni and Skala with their wealth and their famed festivals attract the attention of visitors, Molyvos is a place they must see and experience in order to be able to say that they have got to know the island's character. Next to it is Petra with its monastery clinging to the rock along with its Byzantine and later monuments. The most important archaeological finds in the Bay of Kalloni and Ayia Paraskevi, the amazing beaches of Anaxos, and Eftalou with its therapeutic spa, serve simply to crown this living monument of the Middle Ages which is the historic continuation of ancient Methymna. The shores trod thousands of years ago by Achilles as he moved in to occupy the town are now visited by thousands of tourists every year. Whether the visitor has much or little time at his disposor he must tour the northern part of the island because this region, which has inspired artists and people of intellect for thousands of years, is worth the effort and rewards all those who get to know it.

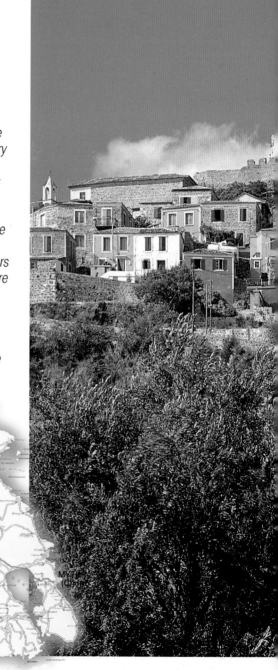

Molyvos, the medieval town.

Lambou Myloi - Ayia Paraskevi

The western exit from the town of Mytilene leads you through olive groves and cultivated fields to the "Loutra of Korfos" and from there to the settlement of **Lambou Myloi** near the river that traverses the region. The village took its name from the water mills that were driven by the water of the Evergetoulas river (mylos = mill). These mills were the nucleus of the development of the early village. The Roman aqueduct also carried water from the river; a section of it still exists west of the village and can be visited, as can the beautiful site of Ayioi Angeloi ("Holy Angels"). Continuing your excursion to the west, on your left you come to a secondary road in the area of Achladeri near which, at the mouth of the Vouvaris river, are the ruins of the ancient town of Pyrra, submerged in the Bay of Kalloni and visible only when the water is calm. A submerged ancient town is an awesome sight and should not be missed, and the ruins of an Early Christian basilica have also been found in the area.

Returning to the main road and continuing on your way to Kalloni, you come to the districts of "Petres to Arabi" ("Black Man's Stones") and "Kryoneri" ("Cold Water") and immediately afterward, passing through the famed pine forest of Tsamliki, you reach the salt-works of the Bay of Kalloni which have been in operation since at least 480 B.C. and today are among the largest in Greece.

On your right is a turn-off to Ayia Paraskevi, a picturesque village that took its name from the small church of Ayia Paraskevi which is built within a rock. **Ayia Paraskevi** was and still is a powerful economic and cultural center on the island and has preserved its characteristics, traditions and customs untouched. That is why its Festival of the Bull, to which extensive reference has been made in another part of this book, is renowned; also characteristic is Carnival, celebrated on the first day of Greek Lent, called "Clean Monday".

Ruins of an Early Christian basilica in the area of Chalinados, near Ayia Paraskevi.

Kalloni

The Kremasti bridge.

Kalloni is next (40 km.). This town has been known by the same name since at least 1300 B.C. It has been one of the most important centers on the island from antiquity till the present with marvellous architecture that one can enjoy when walking through it. The Tsiknias river

In the village there is a cultural center housed in the renovated building of an old olive press which also contains a noteworthy folklore collection worthy of a visit. In the district, outside the settlement of Napi 3 km. later where there is an impressive church to Ayios Ioannis Theologos (St. John the Theologian), there are also a host of other nearby areas with sites worth seeing: at Klopedi the ruins of an ancient temple done in the Aeolian style, are unique in Greece, and reveal the position held by this place, one of the most important in the history of ancient Lesvos. The region also contains the ruins of a Byzantine fortress. At Messa the ruins of a large temple to Aphrodite have been discovered as well as the ruins of an Early Christian basilica from the 5th century B.C. The remnants of buildings from Early Christian times can also be found at Chalinados while at Gerna there are the ruins of an old village. Finally, on the road that connects Ayia Paraskevi to Stypsi in the north, there is an old bridge over the Tsiknias river with legends connected to it that are reminiscent of those surrounding the bridge of Arta; this is the **Kremasti Bridge**.

You return to the main road and, staying in the pine woods, you reach **Arisvi** which has now become one with Kalloni. The village has kept the ancient name of Arisvi, an Aeolian town, whose ruins the archaeological pick has brought to light.

once flowed through the town but is now covered over. Above the bed of the river is where the present-day center of Kalloni is, and it buzzes with life both because of its position on the island and because of the fertile plains which for thousands of years have supplied the inhabitants with their basic commodities, such as the unique black, sweet wine of the area which must by all means be tried. The interesting sight in the town itself is the church of Zoodochos Pigi ("Life-Giving Source"), built in 1805, and the entire area surrounding Kalloni is full of monuments and the ruins of buildings from all periods, a tangible proof of the continual prosperity of the area.

Skala Kallonis

To the south is **Skala Kallonis** which you reach by passing through the settlements of Ariana, Kerami and Papiana, all located in a fertile plain which ends at the rich waters of the bay. Skala has developed into a tourist resort and the festivals that are celebrated there in August at its beautiful harbor, such as the "Festival of the Sardine" and the "Celebration of Reunion", held for the emigrants from the area, on the 16th of the month, attract a host of local and foreign visitors from throughout the world.

Kalloni - Parakoila - Agra

On the west side of the Bay of Kalloni is
Parakoila (52 km.) a settlement that has
been developed for tourism; it lies amid
orange groves in the fertile plain of the area.
From there a secondary road sets off for
Agra (70 km.) a mountainous livestock-
raising village. At the sites of "Makara" and
"Apothika" are the ruins of prehistoric walls
and there are also lovely, tranquil beaches
where you can enjoy the island's sparkling
clean sea.

Images of Skala Kallonis.

Stypsi - Lafionas

Leaving Kalloni you pass the road to Petra and Mithymna in the north of the island. The area is filled with olive groves and pine forests and is one of the most beautiful landscapes on the island. On your left you pass the elevation of Klapados, where the final act in the clash of the Greeks and Turks took place in 1912 and led to the subsequent liberation of the island. Immediately afterward you will arrive at a junction with the road to the village of **Stypsi** on the western slopes of Mt. Lepetymnos. This small village is a typical example of a picturesque mountain village and is well worth a visit. Moreover, there are the ruins of a small medieval castle at the site called Kastreli. Returning to the main road, about 10 km. on from Kalloni you reach the secondary road to **Lafionas**

which is built on a densely wooded hill on the north side of Mt. Skoteinos. The district is of archaeological interest for Ionic capital columns have been found here which testify to the existence of an ancient temple. There are also the ruins of an Early Christian basilica at the site called Ayios Alexandros.

Petra

Back on the main road once more, you get a view of **Petra** (55 km.) from on high; this was the mythical anchorage of Achilles during the Trojan War. The settlement is built on the seaside and around the famous rock from which it takes its present name (petra= rock). You will see a massive rock which appears to have fallen from the sky; it rises to a height of around 30 m. and has the church of the Panayia Glykofilousa (Virgin Mary of the Sweet Kiss) perched on its top; it was built in 1747 and renovated in 1840. There is a stairway with 114 steps leading to the church which has an impressive carved wooden iconostasis as well as an icon of the Virgin Mary. According to a legend, in the 16th century a freighter from Galaxeidi anchored for the night at the small islands opposite Petra. The icon of the Virgin Mary was on the boat. During the night the icon disappeared and at the same time the sailors on the boat observed a glow on the top of the rock. After searching for the icon on top of the rock the following morning and finding it there, they took it back to the ship. But the inexplicable phenomenon happened again, convincing them to leave the icon on the rock in accordance with Divine Will. They immediately began to build the present church.

In the church there is an exhibit of Byzantine ecclesiastical items, open to the public. There is also an impressive feast held in Petra on 15 August in honor of the Virgin Mary, at which a strict observance of the customs of Lesvos creates an image that captivates foreigners.

The stairway which leads to the rock with the church of the Panayia Glykofiloussa.

The settlement of Petra, with its magnificent mansions, is also home to the church of Ayios Nikolaos (St. Nikolas) which is near the enormous plane tree of the village. This is a single-aisled basilica from the 17th century whose interior is completely covered with wall paintings done in three different bands and from different periods. It is conjectured that the present church was the women's loft of an older church which probably was damaged by an earthquake (just like the present one, in 1944). The church floor is lain with tiles while its gilt wooden iconostasis, which is covered with marvellous icons, the oldest being 500 years old, and the bishop's throne, demonstrate in the clearest and most eloquent way that wood-carving is the ecclesiastical art par excellence and together with the artistic marble candelabra dazzle the visitor to this humble little church. The wall painting that stands out is the rare, and perhaps unique, depiction of Judas hanging himself. The celebration in honor of St. Nikolas on 6 December draws many of the faithful from throughout the island and is conducted with particular splendor. The ecclesiastical monuments and the sights in the village of Petra are complemented by the large church of Ayios Georgios (St. George), a triple-aisled basilica built in 1888, the main material being grey trachyte. But Petra also has, among other things, a very important monument which takes one back to the time when the towers were dominant on Lesvos and to the conditions and factors of life during that period. This is the Vareltzidaina Mansion, a western Macedonian type of house, built in 1740. Maintained and open to the public, it is a characteristic example of the tower building of that period. The ground floor, made of stone, without any windows but with a large door, was the storeroom. Around the courtyard were the stables and the other auxiliary spaces needed by the mansion. The stone construction was continued on the first floor but only in those rooms that had a fireplace; the rest of it was built of wood with trapdoors both for communication with the ground floor and for defense.

1

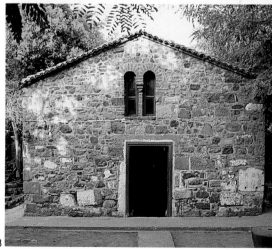

2

1. The Panayia Glykofiloussa.
2.3. The church of Ayios Nikolaos.
4. The Vareltzidaina mansion. 3

4

The exterior wooden staircase forms a pulpit-like structure on the floor where the owner stood during working hours to keep an eye on things. This is also where visitors left their shoes before entering the house. A characteristic example of the customs of the period is the throne in the bedroom. The wall paintings that have been preserved in the women's sitting room as well as the carved wooden ceiling, ornament the interior of the mansion while on the exterior there are two projecting rooms ("sachnisia") and between them a wooden balcony.

Below: The enchanting sunset at Petra and its beautiful beach.
1. 2. 3. Images from the beach at Anaxos.

Paralia Petras - Anaxos - Petri

Outside the bay of Petra, are the islets of Ayios Georgios and Pseira which frame the most beautiful sunsets, and must be experienced by anyone who visits the island. Moreover, it is not by chance that tourist traffic is increasing by leaps and bounds and with it the infrastructure of the area is improving at an equally rapid rate. That is why the beaches of **Petra** and **Anaxos** are filled with people every summer, but the peace and quiet of the simple villages of Lesvos is still to be found in neighboring **Petri**, a picturesque settlement nestled in greenery.

1

2

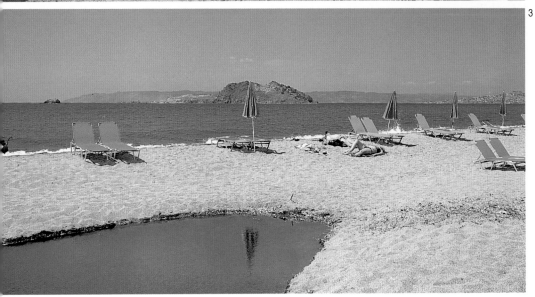

3

Mithymna (Molyvos)

Continuing on to the north, you reach **Molyvos** (Mithymna), perhaps the most picturesque place on the island and at the same time one of the most beautiful locales that Greece has to offer from the medieval period, on a par with Monemvasia in the Peloponnese. Clinging to the slopes of the hill, crowned by its castle, it immediately captivates anyone who sees it for the first time. Drawing near, one can make out the mansions with their "sachnisia" and their multicolored doors and window frames. You pass over the double bridge with the church of Ayios Ignatios (St. Ignatius) and reach the crossroads leading to the town, while to the right a road leads to the castle and the beach at Eftalou.

Since antiquity, Methymna has been an inspiration to artists. The hometown of the cithara virtuoso Arion as well as the modern Greek poet Argyris Eftaliotis, and the place where the writer Ilias Venezis lived, it has developed into an important tourist resort and during the summer the number of its inhabitants increases more than ten-fold.

Down by the sea the harbor of Molyvos is rimmed with shops all around, and the Turkish fountain and the building housing the Harbor-Masters' office are found there, while at the end of the harbor there is a boatyard that is still operational. The old olive press building, that has been converted into a hotel, is truly lovely. A road leads from the harbor to the splendid pebbled beach of Molyvos with its shops and places to eat.

The breakwater is suitable for a stroll, particularly in the late afternoon at sunset when the lights of the village come on, creating a work of art. The finale comes with the illumination of the castle. There are also sea caves near the harbor which can be visited by boat.

Picturesque Molyvos,
which has inspired artists since antiquity.

Sunset in the little harbor of Molyvos.

Many uphill streets set off from the harbor
with a narrow lane leading to the village
market higher up on the slopes. There is
the large covered gallery with a mosque
above it, a busy area with all its shops and
traditional cafes. The numerous fountains
built of red and brown trachyte give this
area a different flavor, reminiscent of the
old days if one lets his imagination run free.
In the center of Molyvos is the paternal
home of Argyris Eftaliotis, at which can be
found his bust, and quite a number of other
important mansions, the most noteworthy
being those of Yiannakos and Krallis.
Indeed the latter is the property of the
School of Fine Arts. The burned ruins of the
house of the heroine in the Greek novel
"The Teacher with the Golden Eyes" by
Stratis Myrivilis can still be found there.
The Town Hall of Mithymna houses an
important archaeological collection, which
is open to the public and contains exhibits
from Greek antiquity to Roman times.
There are also noteworthy exhibits at the
Municipal Gallery and the Public Library.
The churches of the town are of
considerable interest: the Taxiarchis
(Archangel) built in 1795, Ayia Kyriaki,
and Ayios Panteleimonas (St. Panteleimon),
all have special neoclassical features.
Also of significance are the ruins of ancient
Methymna which have survived up to the
present, the main attraction being the
polygonal walls from the 8th century B.C.
and the ancient temple.

*Images from the harbour,
the lanes and the market of Mithymna.*

The **Castle** which stands guard over the area from on high was built during the Byzantine period and reinforced by the Venetian Francesco Gattelusi. It is the best preserved fortress on Lesvos and today has been made over into a facility for cultural events with a dais and a theater pit in the interior. But it is worthwhile passing through the three successive gates and then strolling along the ramparts if for nothing more that the enchanting view and the unique Aegean sunsets.

Eftalou - Vafeio

The road that goes to the castle continues on to the beach at Eftalou with its therapeutic springs, 3 km. away. **Eftalou**, from which Argyris Eftaliotis took his pen name (his real surname: Michaelidis), has developed into a tourist resort. Finally, another road from Molyvos leads to **Vafeio**, a small, picturesque mountain settlement on the slopes of Mt. Lepetymos.

The little harbor of Mithymna.   *1. The Castle.   2. The beach at Eftalou.*

1

2

10

WESTERN LESVOS

Leimonos Monastery - Antissa - Sigri - Eressos

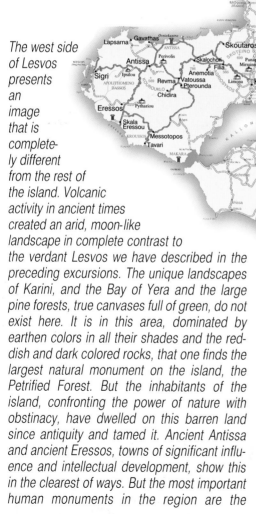

The west side of Lesvos presents an image that is completely different from the rest of the island. Volcanic activity in ancient times created an arid, moon-like landscape in complete contrast to the verdant Lesvos we have described in the preceding excursions. The unique landscapes of Karini, and the Bay of Yera and the large pine forests, true canvases full of green, do not exist here. It is in this area, dominated by earthen colors in all their shades and the reddish and dark colored rocks, that one finds the largest natural monument on the island, the Petrified Forest. But the inhabitants of the island, confronting the power of nature with obstinacy, have dwelled on this barren land since antiquity and tamed it. Ancient Antissa and ancient Eressos, towns of significant influence and intellectual development, show this in the clearest of ways. But the most important human monuments in the region are the

Byzantine monasteries and churches which Orthodoxy founded here, during its most difficult times, for the spiritual training of the monks. This region is full of beautiful and picturesque villages where animal husbandry is the primary occupation. Only at the beginning of the excursion, before reaching Antissa, is there any greenery to be found in the landscape, with a minimum of farming, while Eressos, and more so its port, have been transformed into important tourist resorts which attract more and more visitors who come to savor the same beauties of the island enjoyed by Sappho and Alcaeus. The tour of western Lesvos is most definitely a trip to places that demonstrate the power of nature, but it is at the same time a tour of places where man is waging an ongoing battle to tame it.

The beach at Eressos.

Leimonos Monastery

After Kalloni, and following the road that covers the western part of the island, you first reach the settlement of **Dafia**. A short distance from the village is the historic **Leimonos Monastery**, also called **Taxiarchs**, which has many religious relics and items of national importance among which are the remains of St. Ignatius, and articles of folk art which are exhibited in the museum there. The monastery's library is also a rich one, with more than 2,500 volumes and 450 manuscripts dating from the 9th to the 19th century for it was the main intellectual center on Lesvos during the time of the Turkish occupation, and also possessed a "secret school". There are magnificent wall paintings in the crypt of the main church of the Monastery of Pammegiston Taxarchion (The Almighty Archangels), and the view from the mountain to the Bay of Kalloni is one of unique beauty.

Details and overall view of the Leimonos Monastery.

The first of the monastery's buildings were erected during the period when Byzantium was declining and in 1462 they was destroyed by the Turks. The ruins were purchased by Manuel, the father of St. Ignatius, and the saint brought monastic life back to the island. There is a large celebration held at the monastery on the 13th and 14th of October.

North of the village is the **Convent of the Panayia Myrsiniotissa** (the Virgin Mary of Myrsini) which was founded, like the Leimonos Monastery, by St. Ignatius in 1527 and constituted an annex of the latter. During the period of the Turkish occupation it was where the Greek women on the island fled to escape the Sultan's harems. Today, the nuns produce superb woven goods and rose-water, which you can buy when you visit the monastery. The main church is dedicated to the Dormition of the Virgin Mary. The church of the Panayia (Virgin Mary) is a triple-aisled basilica from 1917, and houses the tomb of St. Ignatius.

View of the village of Skoutaros.

Filia - Skoutaros - Skalochori

Then you reach **Filia** (50 km.), a very beautiful stock-raising village with the architectural features that typify traditional Lesvos, stone houses with roof tiles, rising out of a valley dense with pine and plane trees, oak, walnut and fig trees as well as citrus trees and vineyards. From Filia a secondary road goes to **Skoutaros**.

The main road and a short turn-off takes you to Anemotia, a village famed for its strawberries and grapes, with the imposing church of the Metamorphosis tou Sotiros (The Transfiguration).

Skalochori (58 km.) is the next village you encounter; it has a lovely old school built of locally quarried stone. On the shores north of the village lies ancient Antissa, at Cape Ovriokastro, and there are other ruins from antiquity, in the area of Tsamour (meaning, "good harbor").

The village of Skalochori.

Vatousa - Perivolis Monastery

*Proceeding on to **Vatousa** (67 km.) you will find the interesting churches of the Taxiarch and the Dormition. Near Vatousa, to the south, there are three villages, **Reuma** and **Pterounta**, which have lavish gardens, and **Chydira** the birthplace of the great Greek painter Georgios Iakovidis. As you approach Antissa, you pass on your right, alongside the bed of the Voulgaris river, the **Perivolis Monastery**, built at the beginning of the 17th century, with wall paintings in the Byzantine style. To the west and south the landscape suddenly changes. The characteristic dense vegetation of the rest of Lesvos now gives way to a moon-like landscape where dark-colored, massive rocks predominate.*

*Immediately after the Perivolis Monastery, a turn-off to the right leads to **Gavathas**, the port of modern Antissa, which outside the beautiful sea it has to offer, is also home to two churches subject to preservation: Ayios Vasileios and Ayios Georgios.*

Antissa - Ypsilou Monastery

Antissa (76 km.), built on the barren north slopes of Mt. Kourkoulos, is on the same site as ancient Antissa, which gave birth to the poet Terpander and was destroyed by the Romans in 168 B.C. Today it is a simple market town which lives off animal husbandry and tourism. The Folklore Collection in the district's Cultural Center is of interest. Near the town is the settlement of Tsithra, where one can see interesting wall paintings in the church of Ayios Nikolaos. Five kilometers from Antissa, on the road to Sigri, is the **Ypsilou Monastery**, *at the top of a mountain. Built in 1101, it had 3,000 steps, but these have been replaced by a road. The old church of the monastery was reduced to ashes in 1834 and the present one was built in 1967. The main church of the monastery is dedicated to Ayios Ioannis Theologos (St. John the Theologian) and there is a celebration honoring his name day on 8 May. The monastery has a museum with many relics.*

The Ypsilou Monastery.

Petrified Forest

You have now reached the famous **Petrified Forest** *of Lesvos. Nature has bestowed on the island a unique geological phenomenon, one that causes the visitor to experience a true sense of awe. 15 or 20 million years ago the area was covered with dense sub-tropical vegetation, consisting of enormous trees which reached incredible heights like those of the Sequoia family today found on the American continent, up to 160 meters high, as well as conifers, pines, oak, and cinnamon trees to name only a few. This vegetation was suddenly covered by lava, volcanic ash and tons of earth during powerful volcanic explosions. The abundant water, still found on the island today, in combination with the siliceous union of the lava and the ash, which belched out of the island's volcanoes, (the position of which we are still ignorant of today), petrified the trunks of these trees. Later, rainfall and perhaps seismic activity in the district again brought this ancient forest to the surface, but in a new form.*

There are still some standing fossilized trunks with a circumference of up to 8 meters and a height of up to 6.5 m., masses that are multi-colored and polished, eternal monuments to the power of nature.

The Petrified Forest stretches along the whole western end of the island and since the middle of the 20th century has been known worldwide. This means it is visited by thousands of tourists yearly, but it also means the space is endangered so ATTENTION: it is forbidden to break-off and/or to remove any piece of the petrified forest. Violators will be tried and face many months of imprisonment.

*The Petrified Forest,
a unique geological monument.*

Sigri

Continuing on, you descend to **Sigri**,
the harbor used in times past, which was
protected both by the islets to the west
(the largest being Nisiope) and the small
fortress next to the sea. A highly frequented
summer resort today it has a good tourist
infrastructure and lovely sand beaches.
The sunset at Sigri is a magical event with
the sun disappearing into the waters of the
Aegean, a sight which is unforgettable.
The castle in the harbor is a well-maintained
Turkish building from 1757 built on the ruins
of the Gattelusi's Venetian fortress. There
are also other Byzantine and medieval
buildings in the area, at the location called
Palaiokastro.

*Sigri, the beautiful coastal village
on the western side of Lesvos.*

The boundless beach of Skala Eressou.

Eressos - Skala Eressou

You return to the junction with the road to Antissa and turn right. Soon you will see **Eressos** on your right, the home town of Sappho, the greatest of ancient poetesses, and Theophrastes. The village adds a picturesque note to the barren landscape with its stone houses and the large plane tree in the square. Worthy of note is the Ereipionas (lite-rally, "Ruined Place") where the church is all that is left of the Monastery of Ayios Georgios. On the other side of the road there is a secondary road to the **Pythariou Monastery**, 4 km. to the east. The monastery was founded in the 17th century and is located in a ravishingly beautiful landscape, rare for that area, with plane trees and poplars next to the Chalandra river.
Left of the main road another turn-off leads to **Mesotopos** and, moving down a verdant road with a canopy of trees you reach **Skala Eressou**.

1. The village of Eressos.
2. 3. Skala Eressou.

Skala Eressou, with its superb sand beach, its night spots with wooden stands on the sand and its high quality tourist infrastructure, has developed into an important summer resort center. The cosmopolitan life in summer attracts many tourists who come to enjoy the sun and the sea as well as the hospitality of Lesvos, presented in the best possible way.

Furthermore, large numbers of homosexual women from throughout the world, who idolize the ancient poetess Sappho, regularly gather at Eressos every summer giving the area a global flavor. This is a district that still boasts a few of its ancient glories: ancient Eressos, with its stadium, theater, agora, prytaneum, and the temples of Dionysos, Poseidon, Apollo and Athena, with the harbor and settlement which has spread back from the beach (the sites of the ancient and the new harbor are identical) up to the site of Xokastro on the slopes of the hill where most of the finds were discovered.

At the site of Vigla, on a pine-wooded hill NE of Skala, sections of the walls of the ancient acropolis have been found as well as a prehellenic gate, probably part of a fortification work. South of Vigla are the remnants of a Roman reservoir and next to it the ruins of two towers, one Venetian and the other Turkish. There are even the ruins of the Early Christian basilicas of "Afentelis" with its lovely mosaics and Ayios Andreas (St. Andrew), situated next to another two churches of the same name: one contains the saint's tomb and the other is a modern triple-aisled basilica from 1936-1952. Behind them is the Archaeological Museum which houses important finds from the area, dating from antiquity to the Greek War of Independence of 1821.

The cosmopolitan Skala Eressou offers comforts even the most demanding visitor will enjoy.

Useful Information

How to go

By air *Lesvos is connected to Athens throughout the year by Olympic Airlines. The flight takes 45'. Information may be obtained from the main offices of Olympic Airlines in Athens (tel: 9363363) and in Mytilene (tel. 26565, 28659). There are also many other flights both with other Greek companies and charter flights from Europe and the rest of the world, going to Lesvos airport (tel. 61490, 61590) to cover the needs of tourists.*

By sea *Lesvos has a heavy schedule of connections with the harbors of Piraeus and Rafina in summer and less frequent ones in winter. The distance is covered in 9-12 hours. Information on schedules may be obtained from the Harbor Master's offices of Piraeus (tel. 4226000) and Rafina (tel. 0294-22487, 22300).*

FROM LESVOS

By air Lesvos is connected to Athens, Thessaloniki, Chios and Limnos.
By ship there are connections to the other islands of the NE Aegean, the Dodecanese, the Cyclades and well as the coast of Asia Minor.

Accommodations

HOTELS

The island has a hotel dynamic of over 6,000 beds in more than 100 hotel units which cover all categories from deluxe to the simplest and most economic, but of the same high quality. There are hotels throughout the island so you can choose exactly where you want to stay.

PENSIONS - ROOMS TO RENT

The many pensions and countless rooms to rent host a large number of visitors every year and combine the most economic form of accommodations with a life near the locals, their customs and hospitality.

CAMPING

For those who would prefer a closer relationship with the sun and sea of Lesvos there are two camping sites on the island, MITHYMNA in Molyvos (tel. 71079) and DIONYSOS at Vatera (tel. 61340, 61151-4).

Market

Lesvos has a continually developing market. The variety of goods and services offered is truly inexhaustible, capable of luring even the most conservative shopper both to traditional and tourist items, as well as contemporary articles. Special mention must be made of the island's famous ouzo, the finest in the world according to many. The tradition of centuries has given the island this gift which you should sample from the local producers or from the internationally known bottling companies in Lesvos.

Useful Phone Numbers

For any need that may arise the people at the Tourist Police are the ones most qualified to be of assistance whether you need information or a solution to an economic, legal or other problem. Their offices are located at the harbor of Mytilene (tel. 22776). Lesvos also possesses a superb health system beginning with first aid services and medical care at the General Hospital of Mytilene (tel. 43777) and extending to many private doctor's offices, covering all specializations, as well as many pharmacies throughout the island. There are Health Centers at Antissa (56440-2), Kalloni (tel. 22222), Plomari (tel. 32151) and Polichnitos (tel. 41111).

POST OFFICE

The post office on Lesvos has a complete network of branches and well as participating shops, at which you can send or receive letters and postal money orders and use all the modern postal services. The main offices of ELTA (The Greek Post Office) are at a Vournazon St. in Mytilene (tel. 28823).

OTE (GREEK PHONE COMPANY)

OTE has a complete network of branches on the island in combination with many public card telephones.

In the main offices, which are located on 8 Vournazon St. (tel. 47299), besides facilities for local, long distance and international calls, you will many useful services such as telephone checks and telegrams.

BANKS - EXCHANGE

In Mytilene and other towns on Lesvos there are branches of most of the Greek banks for the servicing of your financial needs. There are also certain shops for the exchange of foreign currency into drachmas.

List of Banks

Mytilene

Agricultural Bank	24081, 23300
National Bank	28651, 20363, 40707
National Mortgage Bank	26810, 27203
Commercial Bank	28172, 27382
General Bank	20961, 23600
Ionian Bank	27650, 25015
Credit Bank	21827, 26759

Kalloni

Agricultural Bank	23379, 23134
National Bank	22103, 22588
Commercial Bank	23215, 23392

Molyvos

National Bank	71210, 71977

Plomari

Agricultural Bank	32675, 31320
National Bank	32305, 32205
Commercial Bank	32404, 32204

Telephone Codes Lesvos:

Mytilene, Thermi, Loutra	0251
Plomari, Ayiassos, Polichnitos, Yera	0252
Kalloni, Molyvos, Antissa, Sigri, Eressos, Mantamados, Ayia Paraskevi	0253